I0517991

Refreshing the Saints

Favorite Old Testament Texts

Onesimus Bible Study Series

Edited by
Bill Bagents

CYPRESS
PUBLICATIONS
An Imprint of Heritage Christian University Press

Published by Cypress Publications

Copyright © 2024 by Bill Bagents

Manufactured in the United States of America

Cataloging-in-Publication Data

Refreshing the saints: favorite Old Testament texts/edited by Bill Bagents

p. cm.

Includes scripture index.

ISBN 978-1-956811-67-4(pbk.); 978-1-956811-68-1 (ebook)

1. Bible. Old Testament—Study and teaching. 2. Christian life—Study and teaching. I. Bagents, William Ronald, 1956–, editor. II. Title.

221.007—dc20

Library of Congress Control Number: 2024942793

Cover design by Brad McKinnon and Brittany Vander Maas.

All rights reserved. No part of this publication may be reproduced, distributed, stored in a retrieval system, or transmitted in any form or by any means without the prior written permission of the publisher, except in the case of brief quotations embodied in critical reviews and certain other noncommercial uses permitted by copyright law.

For information:

Cypress Publications

3625 Helton Drive, PO Box HCU, Florence, AL 35630

www.hcu.edu

Onesimus Bible Study Series

The Onesimus Bible Study Series offers biblical lessons for personal or group study from alumni of International Bible College / Heritage Christian University. Each lesson flows from confidence in Scripture as God's inspired, living, and powerful word. Each respects the ongoing relevance of the Bible as it shows us God's heart and guides our service in the name of Jesus. Every lesson is designed to build faith and encourage Christian living.

Why the name Onesimus? We love the brief book of Philemon, in which Onesimus shines as a stunning example of trusting God more than self or circumstance. The runaway slave met the apostle Paul and encountered God's truth. Out of respect for God—and with Paul's blessing and support—Onesimus chose to return to his owner. He did right by obeying the unfortunate and challenging law of the day despite potentially heavy costs and consequences.

Many of our alumni write beautifully. They also exhibit the servant's heart modeled by Onesimus. Their loyalty to God and submission to Scripture model the faithful excellence of Onesimus. We're blessed to know and serve with such fine brethren. We believe they will bless you too.

Editors of Heritage Christian University Press

Contents

Chapter 1
The Creation Account
Genesis 1
Gary G. Payne

FOCUS PASSAGE

Genesis 1:1 through 2:3, "In the beginning God created the heavens and the earth . . . ."

ONE MAIN THING

Our Creator continues creating—making you new in Christ as He is forming the New Heaven and Earth.

INTRODUCTION

The Bible begins with an explosive vision. We cannot fathom an existence beyond what we know. We cannot understand an existence where there is no matter and no light. Infinity is beyond what we know. Then, in the biblical text, something more than nuclear crashes through the unknown, and from a Force that is beyond anything we can explain the Cosmos comes into being.

Suddenly there is order. There is life. There is goodness. There is the Creator and His Creation.

The Creation account in Genesis 1 is foundational for the rest of Scripture. The Bible is full of citations and allusions from Genesis 1. Quite often, the Creation account shaped the way biblical writers expressed truths. Biblical writers did not just make stuff up. They heard their history passed down from generation to generation. They learned about the Creator and how the Creation is a sacred gift. They learned how humans are a part of the Creator's plan as He continues to create something new.

GOING DEEPER

Consider how we understand God. Our imagination tries to capture a snapshot of what the power of God might be like. In movies, there are bolts of lightning, frightening crashes of thunder, and unbearable earthquakes. Even the Bible uses these scenes on Mount Sinai or with trumpets blowing in the Book of Revelation. Still, the images do not do justice to the awesome power unleashed when God speaks on each Creation Day. His power is incompressible. We serve a mighty God!

God is completely Other.[1] He is past understanding. His Otherness is even more heightened when one considers the doctrine of the Trinity. In Genesis 1, God speaks. In Genesis 1:2, the Spirit hovers over the waters. In Genesis 1:26, God says, "Let *us* make man in *our* image, in *our* likeness" (italics mine).[2] The New Testament names Jesus as the Creator.[3] Theologians attempt to explain the Trinity—three Persons who are one God. I do not know any adequate explanations. My best recommendation is to embrace the Mystery. The Almighty Creator is beyond our comprehension.

Yet, in saying that God is completely Other, there is an irony. Our Creator had to be near to create. The literary structure for Genesis 1 gives a sense of order, harmony, and balance.[4] God is in complete control and is sustaining what He made. Each day God observes what He made, and it is good. The world He made is fundamentally good—another indicator that God is close and connected. Then He creates humans on the sixth day. God looks at the entire Creation and it is "very good" (1:31). People are the pinnacle of His Creation—His crowning achievement. That should be very encouraging to everyone reading this.

So, God creating shows how near He is to us. I heard one preacher explain that for God to make Adam out of dirt means God got dirty. He loves us that much and gets that close to us. That brings us to another consideration: Genesis 1 gives us God's view of how to understand human beings. Living creatures, including humans, are alive because God breathes the "breath of life" in them (Gen 1:30). This makes life sacred. All life. This does not mean God expects us to be vegetarians. After all, He made provisions in the Scriptures for eating meat. However, we do approach our meals with thanksgiving. That's because we know that the animal we are eating is a sacred gift from God to us. The same is true for the animals God gave to clothe Adam and Eve (Gen 3:21). That animal previously had the breath of life from God. Animals are sacred gifts from God and His gifts are not to be taken lightly. Now, if an animal's life is sacred, how much more is a human life?! Our life is holy because we have God's "breath of life" to make our bodies live. Then, we have an added feature: God made us in His image (Gen 1:27).[5]

Genesis 1 presents us with amazing imagery showing us the Creator, His Creation, and the sacred life He brought to be—especially in humanity. Now this marvelous tapestry begins to grow into a message that is timeless. Genesis 1 is the foundation for the Double Love Command. The Shema is the greatest command: "Hear, O Israel: The LORD our God, the LORD is one. Love the LORD your God with all your heart and with all your soul and with all your strength" (Deut 6:4-5). Knowing that our Creator, who is completely Other, loves us enough to be near drives us to complete devotion. The second greatest command is like the first: "Love your neighbor as yourself. I am the LORD" (Lev 19:18). Since humans embody the sacred, it matters how we treat each other. In essence, how we treat each other is a reflection of how we treat God.[6] This makes these two commands inseparable. Jesus even says that on these two commands hang "all the Law and the Prophets" (Matt 22:40).[7] The Double Love Command is the force that will shape society. God is love. Those who love God will love others. The prophets longed for a day when God's ideal for social justice would be the hallmark of God's kingdoms presence on earth.[8]

In Genesis 1, God created something new. However, God did not stop after resting on the seventh day. God remains fully engaged in His Creation, continuing to create things new, continuing to bring about possibilities, and forging ahead to the redemption of all things.[9] The biblical messengers who brought us God's Word through the ages experienced a creating God who is fully engaged in human affairs. When Noah and his family stepped out of the Ark, there was a new creation. When God used Moses to free His people from Egypt, the Exodus began the process of a new creation—the birth of a nation that would one day bring forth the Messiah. When God freed His people from Babylonian Captivity, this new Exodus was also a re-creation of the Nation of Israel so God would continue His plan to bring the Messiah. The birth, death, resurrection, and ascension of Jesus and the establishment of His church as the new Israel was a new creation. Now we look to the day when God will usher in the New Heaven and New Earth. Our God is in the creation business. It all started in Genesis 1. God's creative redemption work has been a tremendous encouragement for the Saints for all time through all ages.

APPLICATION

Genesis 1 brings us into a realm of mystery. How can one fathom the complete "otherness" of God, His great power, and how there are Three in One (the Trinity)? Then, who can imagine that the Almighty would then be so near that He would care enough to create us, breathe into us life, and make us in His image? Such a realization brings people to know pure Love and pure worship.

So then, God extends something of Himself into the essence of every human being. For those of us who know that, we change how we treat each other. We treat others as if there is something divine in the other person—because there is. We become compassionate. We become serving. We seek justice. We are merciful.

God is changing how we see Him and how we treat others. He is transforming His Creation. This is God making things new. This is God creating the New Heaven and New Earth. The Scriptures say that Jesus "is the same yesterday and today and forever."[10] I suspect when the New Heaven and New Earth come to be, He will still be creating. As a participant in God's plan, you are a part of something big!

CONCLUSION

This study only scratches the surface. I find Genesis 1 to be among the most encouraging passages in Scripture because the Creation account is foundational for the rest of Scripture. It provides a basis for what we believe, for how we treat each other, and for the hope we have for the life to come. May God bless you as you look forward to God's creative power as He works in you and as He works to usher in the New Heaven and Earth.

DISCUSSION QUESTIONS

1. What can we know about God from the Genesis 1 Creation account?
2. What do we know about people from the Genesis 1 Creation account?

3. How is the Genesis 1 Creation account the basis for social justice?
4. What is the most encouraging part of this study for you? Why?

Endnotes

[1] Denis Baly, *God and History in the Old Testament: The Encounter with the Absolutely Other in Ancient Israel* (New York, NY: Harper & Row 1976).

[2] All citations from Scripture in this chapter are from the New International Version.

[3] See, John 1:1–3, 1:14; Colossians 1:15–20; and, Hebrews 1:6, 1:10–12.

[4] John Willis, editor, *Genesis*, The Living Word Commentary on the Old Testament (Abilene, TX: Abilene Christian University, 1984), 78. Some formatting changes were made to this chart. When considering this chart, keep in mind the balance and harmony that Genesis 1 presents to those who hear it.

The Literary Structure of the Creation Account in Genesis 1:1-2:3			
Introduction—1:1-2			
Habitats		**Creatures**	
Day 1	Light 1:3-5	Day 4	Light Bearers 1:14-19
Day 2	Sky / Water Separated 1:6-8	Day 5	Birds / Fish 1:20-23
Day 3	Dry Land / Vegetation 1:9-13	Day 6	Land Animals / Man 1:24-31
Conclusion—2:1-3			

Furthermore, God's control and sustainment of His Creation is shown with Him "resting" on the seventh day. In contrast, in Mesopotamia, the 7th, 14th, and 28th days of the month were "unlucky." These were their Sabbath days. These were the days when the world was at the most risk. The goddess Tiamat—"the deep"— would potentially rear her ugly head and destroy the world. Contrast that with Genesis 2:2: "By the seventh day God had finished the work he had been doing; so on the seventh day he rested from all his work." For those believing in God as Creator, there was no fear. The Sabbath was blessed. "The world falling apart on the Sabbath? Right! Our God even *rests* on that day. We don't have to worry about our world falling apart. God is holding it together."

[5] Consider King David's proclamation that he was fearfully and wonderfully made (Ps 139:13–16). Also, contemplate passages such as the Ten Commandments where we are told, "Do not kill."

[6] Consider Matthew 25:31–46.

[7] See also Matthew 7:12.

[8] In Israel's history up to 3,000 years ago, Amos, Hosea, Micah, Isaiah, Nahum, Habakkuk, and others messaged dignity and respect for all people. They preached against the powerful and the rich exploiting others. They spoke about providing a voice for those with no voice. They demanded care for the widows, orphans, and the poor. The prophet Micah (6:8) sums it up like this:

He has showed you, O man,

What is good.
And what does the LORD
Require of you?
To act justly and to love mercy
And to walk humbly with your God.

[9] Romans 8:18–25.
[10] Hebrews 13:8.

Chapter 2
Where Are You?
An Intimacy Reflecting Question on Your Walk with God: Genesis 3:8–15
Hong An Tran

Focus passage: Genesis 3:8–15

They heard the sound of the LORD God *walking* in the garden in the cool of the day, and the man and his wife hid themselves from the presence of the LORD God among the trees of the garden. But the LORD God called to the man and said to him, 'Where are you?"[1]

Introduction

"Where are you?" demonstrates divine love, a simple yet profound question that encapsulates the essence of our relationship with God. God's question to the first couple reveals the depth of our *needs*, the magnitude of our *problems*, and the grace of the *opportunities* for our redemption.

Adam and Eve stand out among the biblical figures

who have walked with God. The term 'walking with God' is not explicitly used in our text, as with Enoch (5:24) or subsequent patriarchs (Noah, Abraham, etc.). How Adam and Eve walk with God uniquely reflects a perfect and intimate relationship with God *before* and *after* the fall.

Going Deeper

The narratives in Genesis 1–3 are not just historical (Matt 19:4–5; Luke 3:38; Jude 14), but also a source of divine instruction (2 Tim 3:16–17) and theological insights (Rom 5:14; 1 Cor 15:22, 45; 2 Cor 11:3; 1 Tim 2:13–14). The description of God in human terms (speaking, seeing, calling, and walking) may alert readers not to interpret God literally but *intimately*. Let's discuss our text regarding characters: God, Adam, Eve, and the serpent.

The Serpent

In light of the New Testament (Rev 12:9,15; 20:2; 2 Cor 11:3; John 8:44), there is more to say about the serpent's origin, true identity, and deeds as Satan. However, the serpent is one of God's animal creatures, yet more crafty (1, 14). His wisdom, emphasizing not just the ability to speak but *what* and *how* the serpent would *say* about God's word, threatens human innocence (2:25). The serpent's strategy is to lure people into *distrusting* God and so *disobeying* God's word. Using words instead of force implies how human free will can neutralize or actualize the tactic of temptation (cf. Matt 4:1–10). For this reason, the serpent is responsible for his deeds before God (14). Therefore, it clears the ground for wondering whether he might be a force, non-being, or impersonal evil.

Adam and Eve

In answering the serpent, the woman attempts to defend God's command while restricting herself from *touching* the fruit. According to her words, Adam and Eve were aware of the consequences, even though they had not *yet* experienced death (2:16–17; 3:2–3). The gravity of the consequences incites the woman to over-state God's words, suggesting that a fear of death might have driven the woman's interpretation.

On the other hand, the woman's interpretation has a significant flaw, assuming she intended to reinforce God's command. To illustrate this, imagine that Adam and Eve abstained from eating and even touching the fruit and later passed this *strict* interpretation down to their chil-dren. Suppose one day, out of curiosity or by accident, their son touched the fruit and experienced no immediate consequence. In that case, the son might doubt and ulti-mately reject the original commandment (2:17). Touching the fruit is different from eating it. Thus, in her attempt to safeguard God's words, the woman inadver-tently makes them "less secure," potentially creating confusion and doubt. This innovative approach, though well-intentioned, could be counterproductive.

Nevertheless, it might imply that their relationship

with God was rooted more in fear rather than in love and trust. They might have been so frightened of God or death that they were willing to forsake their freedom to touch the fruit despite God's command, which only forbade eating it. This is reminiscent of the Israelites, who were afraid to hear directly from God and preferred to listen to Moses (Exod 20:18–20). Although both the woman and Adam *believed that* eating the fruit would result in death, the question remains whether they would *trust* God and remain faithful to His word when faced with temptation.

God and His Image

God's questions move from *where* to *who* and *what* (9–13), revealing insights into human needs, problems, and opportunities.

On the surface, the question, "where ..." assumed that God and man have no doubt been walking with one another *before*. Here is the beauty of God's description in human terms, "the sound of God *walking* ... ." Now, God walked *alone* in the garden, while man and his wife hid from God behind the trees, just as they hid from each other behind the fig leaves. It implied that they knew their need to show up for God. So, God must raise His voice to seek them, "Where are you?" God did not punish them immediately when He *found* them. Hence, God's love is seen in how He *walked* with them through His questions to unfold their problems.

On a deeper level, although God is omniscient and knows their physical location, His questions highlight the profound change in humanity's spiritual and relational walk with Him. Adam and the woman were unafraid of God before. There had been no shame in their innocent nakedness physically and spiritually in the presence of each other and God, but now there was. It underscores their current state of disobedience, fear, and separation from God and each other, contrasting sharply with their previous state of innocence and open fellowship.

The question "Who told ..." can be asked differently: Who do you *trust* to learn that you are naked? Trusting God would not result in such shameful awareness. If nobody would provide such knowledge, they must have first committed *distrusting* God and then *disobeying* His words. The former is addressed by the question of *who* and the latter by *what* (11–12).

Now, they *know* that they *need* to be clothed spiritually before God. Sadly, they did admit their deeds but did not seize the opportunity to admit they were wrong before God. Moreover, both decided deliberately to blame God and His creatures for their deeds (Adam blamed the woman and God, and the woman blamed the serpent).

Significantly, God's questions of love were directed *only* to His image–bearers, Adam and the woman. The serpent was not questioned but directly cursed, saturating the contrast between God's image and the rest of His creatures. This is God's grace initiating before the condemnation of death.

God promised grace through the woman's seed by announcing the judgment for the serpent, even before announcing judgment for humanity in order—first to the serpent, then to the woman, and finally to Adam. There-fore, Adam rekindled his trust in God's promise by naming his wife Eve, the mother of all living.

God did not love through *words* only but also through His compassionate and gracious *actions*. God did not drive Adam and Eve out of the garden naked and ashamed; instead, God Himself made garments of skins for them and clothed them (21). Thus, His love covers their nakedness, signifying He will walk them through their problems even outside the garden.

Application

Chapter 3 may be considered a Q&A chapter explaining why everything was perfect initially but not now. Given the conclusion (1:31), we must assert that God is not the author of evil. Evil must come from free moral beings.

The first question of love in human history came from God: "Where are you?" This divine question demonstrates God's great love, manifesting His mercy and grace as He walks *toward* humanity. It reflects the mission of Jesus Christ, who came to seek the lost. God has sent His Son through whom the tree of life is acces-sible again for all who trust God and obey Christ's words (Rev 21–22). Thus, all would walk with God once more time in Christ. The question addresses not only those who are spiritually lost but also every Christian, urging them to rekindle their walk with God.

God seeks us today through His Son with the same question: "Where are you?" How we respond to His love profoundly impacts our walk with God. Through generations, those who walk with God are distinguished and blessed, while those who walk away are cursed and ashamed. We can observe others walking with God from afar or choose to walk with God.

Trust and love should guide us to embrace God's words fully, without distortion or unnecessary additions. When we truly trust and love God, even though we must respectfully fear Him, we will adhere to His words without adding our restrictions. A healthy relationship with God focuses on the positive aspects of being with God rather than the negative aspects of avoiding what is forbidden.

Conclusion

The woman was deceived, and Adam disobeyed God. Both deliberately violated God's command by their own will, introducing sin and death into the world. Nevertheless, God's love found them where they were. He did not abandon them but abounded with His love. In announcing the judgment for the serpent, God implicitly promised hope through the woman's seed, indicating that through this redemptive promise, they could be clothed and walk with Him again.

What a love! What a grace! How and why does God have to go through these painful *questions* and *actions* to help them understand *who* and *what* they have lost? It warms our hearts to read this story, knowing how deeply God loves us and initiates His search for us to establish His redemptive promise. After all, His Son has come to seek us. Should we walk away or walk with God in the cool of the day?

Discussion Questions

1. Will the divine question, "Where are you?" remind you of your walk with God when you leave Him walking alone? How would you respond to such a gracious question?

2. Jesus Christ has become a curse and the righteous robe to redeem our walk with God (Gal 3). Will you trust Jesus Christ for your needs, problems, and opportunities?

3. What could God have done more in words and deeds than what has already been demonstrated in Christ? If there is no greater love than that, will you step forward to demonstrate your love for God?

4. There is no other way of living that is more pleasing to God than walking with Him. Will you walk with God? Remember, walking with God is the path of life and blessing. Who else would you want to walk with if not God? If someone other than God walks with you, what would the outcome or destination of that walk be?

Endnotes

[1] *The Holy Bible*: English Standard Version (Wheaton, IL: Crossway Bibles, 2016), Gen 3:8–15.

Chapter 3
Go!
Genesis 12:1
Rickey Collum

> Now the Lord said to Abram, "Go from your country
> and your kindred and your father's house to the land
> that I will show you" (Gen 12:1 ESV).

SOME MIGHT WONDER WHY, OF ALL THE BEAUTIFUL
verses found in the Old Testament, I would select this
one as my favorite. It has not always been, but it has
continued to grow on me. I find it fascinating that God
would choose a non-believer (Josh 24:2) from Ur, a pagan
city, to "go." Also, Abram left his home, family, and
friends, for an unknown destination and an unsure future
for an unknown God. This is the first example of the
strength of Abram's faith. This is also the beginning of
the journey of God and Abram—a journey that will
reveal the growing pains of their relationship, as well as
the progression of Abram's faith in God and, to a lesser
extent, God's faith in Abram.

When we read this Old Testament verse, we are
reminded of the "go" found in Mark 16:15–16,

And he said to them, "Go into all the world and proclaim the gospel to the whole creation. Whoever believes and is baptized will be saved, but whoever does not believe will be condemned."

The Greek word that is translated as "go" in Mark is the word for travel. We know that we must travel all over the world to seek and save the lost. However, in Genesis 12:1, the phrase in Hebrew for the word "go" could also be translated leave. God is telling Abram to leave his pagan background, his unbelieving family, and his friends so that his faith will grow without outside difficulties.

Of all the men available to an all-knowing, all-seeing God, He chose a middle-aged man who was content, wealthy, upper class, and perhaps pagan to become the "Father of the Faith." So much so that every follower of God from the time of Abram forward will be referred to as "the seed of Abraham" (cf. Rom 4:1–3, 16–24; Gal 3:6–9; Heb 11:8–19; Jas 2:21–23).

In verse 1, the part that states *"Go from your country"* seems a very simple command in which we see a basic Biblical principle for those who would follow God; that is the idea of separation from that which is wicked, unholy, and worldly. Upon further study, the command goes even further to include our need to be set apart, holy, and godly. For example, Paul records a similar command to all New Testament believers which is like the command God made to Abram.

Therefore go out from their midst, and be separate from them, says the Lord, and touch no unclean thing;

then I will welcome you, and I will be a father to you, and you shall be sons and daughters to me, says the Lord Almighty (2 Cor 6:17–18).

Genesis 11:27–32 gives us some clarification about why God wanted Abram to leave Ur. Haran, Abram's brother, died in Ur, "the land of his birth," before the family left (v. 28). Abram married Sarah (Sarai) in Ur, and they lived there long enough for her barrenness to be an established fact prior to departure (vs 29, 30).

Abram lived during Patriarchal times, so Terah, his father, would have been the patriarch or leader of the family. So instead of Abram leading the exodus of Ur, Terah took his family from Ur, and they left "to go into the land of Canaan" (v. 31). We know that Terah led the migration from Ur toward the land of Canaan. However, the migration stopped short of God's intended destination. They settled at Haran, a place that held many things in common with Ur (v. 31). It is possible that Terah used his patriarchal status to prevent Abram from leaving without his family. One point that leans toward this being true is that God did not renew his call to Abraham until after the death of his father (Gen 11:32—12:1; Acts 7:4).

Two other passages give insights into God's call of Abraham at Ur. In his final address Joshua declared to Israel that Terah and their fathers of old times served other gods "beyond the River" (Josh 24:2). If "beyond the River" is to be identified with Ur, Joshua declared that Terah and his family served pagan gods prior to God's call of Abraham. In Stephen's sermon before the

Jewish council, he declared that God's call to Abraham in Ur was the same call Abram received a second time in Haran: he was to leave his land, leave his kindred, and go to a land which God would show him (Acts 7:2–3).

Can you fathom what it would take to have the faith exhibited by Abram from the very beginning? To leave everything you have ever known to go to a place that an unknown God would eventually show you? Still, his faith is a growing faith and has not reached its full potential.

You can observe the setbacks and the growth of Abram's faith in God. You can see Abram's lies, doubt, and questioning, but you also witness the progression of his faith. Yet, Abram's faith was not where God wanted.

I believe the wisdom that Abram used in his confrontation with Lot was the turning point (Gen 13). It is our first view of Abram's faith unaided. God renewed His original promise to Abram (Gen 13:14–18). God proclaimed that all the land that Abram saw would be his and his descendants—and that those descendants would be too many to count.

Many have debated that, when Abram included Lot in his journey from Haran, he defied God because Lot was his nephew. One side upholds that when Lot's father died, Abram according to Jewish custom became his guardian. This would make Lot a part of Abram's immediate family and would not have gone against God's command. The other side affirms that Lot's constant tendency to bring conflict into his uncle's life is ample proof that God did not intend for Lot to be a part of Abram's life. Whichever path you choose, notice that much like Abram's father, God did not offer His divine protection until after Lot was out of the picture.

In my humble opinion, it was when Abram trusted God's promise to deliver a son, even though he was full of doubt, that God recognized Abram's faith.

> And he brought him outside and said, "Look toward heaven, and number the stars, if you are able to number them." Then he said to him, "So shall your offspring be." And he believed the Lord, and he counted it to him as righteousness (Gen 15:5–6).

Nothing physically changed with Sarah. She was no less barren, and Abram had not grown younger. The only thing that changed was the faith that Abram had in God, the righteous faith that it takes to be the "Father of the Faith." In the same way that God chose Abram, a non-believer from a pagan city to go, God chose a barren woman to give birth to a nation that would become the people of God. He wanted to show us the barrenness of Abraham and Sarah, to help us see His glorious power. He made man out of the dust of the earth. He gave birth to the nation of Israel from two barren followers.

Thinking back on Abram's "go" command, it may not have been so difficult. When you examine the "I will" statements found in verses 2 and 3 of Genesis 12. It begins at the end of verse 1 where God states *"I will show you."*

> And *I will make of you* a great nation, and *I will bless you* and make your name great, so that you will be a

blessing. *I will bless those who bless you*, and him who dishonors you *I will curse*, and in you all the families of the earth shall be blessed.

Also, at the end of verse 2, some versions translate *"make you a great name"* into another "I will" statement, *"I will magnify your name."*

When we think of this chapter and these verses, we remember the promise God made to Abram, that he would be the start of a great nation. But upon further examination, we can see the more personal promise God gave to Abram. The promise that God would be with him and would remain with him. God said "Go" and Abram went; he believed the promise, without any visible evidence. He obeyed God. He did not question God. That is faith, even though it is not called that by name here. That is pure faith.

And without faith it is impossible to please him, for whoever would draw near to God must believe that he exists and that he rewards those who seek him (Heb 11:6).

Our Christian lives are often comparable to the journey of Abraham. We must learn to trust God and go when and where he says to go. Sometimes we do not know the destination. Sometimes we must leave friends and family behind, but we must go because He says go! This is the only way to grow your faith. Much like Abraham, this may take time, but the journey begins with a step.

Discussion Questions

1. Discuss, in your life, people or things you left behind so that you could "go" toward God.
2. How are we today considered the "seed of Abraham"?
3. Do we, like Abram's father Terah, sometimes stop short of obeying God's commands?
4. Give examples of different times, in the life of Abraham, when you could see his faith grow.
5. Who are "the people of God" today?

Chapter 4
God Will Provide
Genesis 22:1–19
Brad McNutt

FOCUS PASSAGE

Genesis 22:1–19

INTRODUCTION

Trust. The word contains five letters, one syllable, and is synonymous with "faith," but sometimes it feels nearly impossible to live out. This challenge only increases when living in the information age of fake news, and the notion that truth is relative. Not only is it hard to know what to believe concerning the news, it's even harder to find people that you can completely trust. Friendships and marriages are broken daily because of a violation or lack of trust. Trust is based on the character or trustworthiness of the person in whom you place it. The struggle comes because no one is perfect, and all make mistakes, so there is no human being in whom we can place perfect trust.

The fact that God is perfect makes Him preeminently trustworthy. With Him, our trust is correctly and safely placed. This is why we are admonished to trust God with all our hearts (Prov 3:5–8). However, if we are completely honest with ourselves, we know how incredibly difficult that is. Who among us hasn't looked to the heavens and wondered what God is doing or where He is? Add to this our compulsion to try and "help" God accomplish things we believe should be done. And yet, this (trust) is the foundation (Heb 11:6) and trajectory of Christian life (Rom 1:17).

When I think of trust/faith in God, my mind immediately goes to the patriarch, Abraham. The New Testament writers often portray Abraham as a prime example of trust/faith to Jews and Gentiles (Rom 4:1–25; Heb 11:8–19; Jas 2:21–23). However, looking at the Abraham narrative (Gen 11:27–23:20), it quickly becomes apparent that it took Abraham a long time to trust God completely. In fact, it is said of Abraham early in his journey, "And he believed the LORD and he counted it to him as righteousness." (Gen 15:6). This text is quoted many times in the New Testament. James, presumably the half-brother of Jesus, argued that the above passage (Gen 15:6) found its fulfillment when Abraham offered Isaac as a burnt offering at Mount Moriah (Jas 2:21–23).[1] Thus, in Genesis 22, Abraham finally reaches the pinnacle of trust. A perfect example of his trust is found in his own words when he was asked by Isaac about the sacrificial animal's[2] absence; the patriarch responded, "God will provide for himself the lamb for a burnt offering my son." (Gen 12:8). God will provide. Trust.[3]

GOING DEEPER

The Abraham and Isaac narrative begins with the call of God to sacrifice the beloved son (Gen 22:1–2).[4] The author informs the reader that God is putting Abraham to the test. Notice how Isaac is described as "your son, your only son Isaac, whom you love" (v. 2).[5] This helps the reader to understand that the tension of the story is between the beloved son (vv. 2, 12, 16), the gift, and God, the Giver. Finally, Isaac is to be sacrificed as a burnt offering (v. 2) on Mount Moriah.[6] This would involve not only killing Isaac but also burning his body to ashes (Lev 1).

Upon receiving this revelation from God, perhaps in a dream, Abraham doesn't delay. He is characterized by action: "rose, saddled, took, cut, arose, went" (v. 3).[7] Three days later, upon arrival, Abraham instructs his servants to stay behind while he and Isaac go worship[8] and return (vv. 4–5).[9] With the instructions given, father and son take the necessary items for a sacrificial offering. Isaac thinks the sacrifice is missing, but Abraham knows he has everything he needs, confident that God will provide (vv. 6–8).

As the duo reaches the place of offering, Abraham is again characterized by action: "built, laid, bound, laid, reached, took."[10] (vv. 9–10). As Abraham is about to slaughter his son, the angel of the LORD[11] speaks and stops him from killing Isaac. After halting the beloved son's sacrifice, he says, "... for now I know that you fear[12] God, seeing you have not withheld your son, your only son from me" (v. 12). At this time, God provides just as

Abraham knew he would (v. 8), and he offers the ram in the place of his son and renames the site "the LORD will provide." (v. 14). Abraham had passed the trust test! As a result, God intensified the blessings and promises he previously made (vv. 15–19).[13]

Obviously, the nature of a father sacrificing his son on an altar as a test of faith makes this chapter compelling. It could stand on its own as enthralling literature. However, when placed into its fuller context, it is only intensified. One dominant theme of the Abraham narrative is the promise of a son. It was a centerpiece of the original promise (Gen 12:2). The only problem? Sarah was barren (Gen 11:30) and they were both beyond the years of childbearing. Paul observed that Abraham's body was as good as dead and that Sarah's womb was dead (Rom 4:19). While not the most sensitive way to communicate it, the wording reveals the hopelessness of the picture.

Throughout the narrative, Abraham struggles with this promise of a son. Maybe it will be Lot as an adopted nephew from his deceased brother?[14] Not to be, they part ways (Gen 13:1–18). If not Lot, then surely it will be Eliezer of Damascus who, it seems, was the manager of his household (Gen 15:1–3). But God said it wouldn't be Eliezer but a son from Abraham's own body (Gen 15:4–6). Now that it has been made clear that Abraham's son will come from his body, maybe he can have a son with another woman, namely Hagar (Gen 16:1–6), but that was not to be (Gen 17:18, 21:8–21). God again promised many descendants (Gen 17:1–8) and an heir through Sarah (Gen 17:15–21, 18:9–15). Then, twenty-five years after the original promise (Gen 12:1–3), God provided a son through Sarah (Gen 21:1–4).

As a reader, you would think this is Abraham's life's pinnacle moment.[15] God promised, Abraham struggled and waited, Isaac was born, and all was well. Happily ever after. Or not. He is forced to send Ishmael away (Gen 21:8–21) and then called upon to kill the promised beloved son (Gen 22:1–2). It's amazing that when God made the promise of a son, Abraham struggled mightily to trust God. However, when God called him to sacrifice his beloved son, Abraham trusted without reservation. That's the point. When Abraham told Isaac that God would provide (Gen 22:8), he summarized what had taken him a lifetime to understand: trust God even if He asked you to do something that may not make sense initially.

The command to take the only son of promise—for which he had waited so long and to which all the promises were tied—and kill him would mean that God's promise would have fallen to the ground if he perished. The writer of Hebrews helps us understand Abraham's thinking in that he trusted God and His promises so much that God would raise his son's charred remains from the dead before He would break his word to Abraham (Heb 11:17–19). That wasn't a far reach to him. Remember, Issac was born from a man who was as good as dead, and a woman whose womb was dead (Rom 4:19). His initial birth was a "resurrection" against all odds. Why would his death not be the same? Abraham had learned that God is to be trusted. He always keeps His promises! God always provides!

APPLICATION

Abraham was an ordinary man. When God called him, he was an idolater in the region of Mesopotamia (Gen 11:27–12:3; Josh 24:2, 14–15).[16] He brought him out on an amazing journey of faith. It all began with a decision to leave everything he knew for an unknown future. Over the next one-hundred-plus years (Gen 12:4, 25:7), God proved Himself trustworthy and to always provide. What could He do with you if you were willing to trust him? He will be as patient with you in your mistakes and failures to trust as He was with Abraham. Do you believe that God will provide?

As previously mentioned and readily evident by reading the Abraham narrative, his trust was a work in progress. With all of the mistakes that Abraham made (trying to substitute others as the chosen son, lying about his wife, and questioning God's promises), God never berated him or beat him over the head. What did God do? He continued to provide, bless, and assure Abraham. Why wouldn't He do the same for you? Whatever you are struggling with, trust Him and watch Him take you to higher and higher levels of trust until you, too, say like Abraham in the face of great trial, "God will provide" (Gen 22:8).

CONCLUSION

Trust. The word contains five letters, one syllable, and is synonymous with "faith." It sometimes seems impossible, but according to Abraham, it is doable. Abraham walked with God for a long time. As they went together, God provided every step of the way. A great God who has proven trustworthy is the foundation of trust. As Christians, God has provided for our greatest need by giving us His son. After seeing that, is there anything that He won't provide? (Rom 8:31–39) Is there any reason for us not to trust Him completely?

DISCUSSION QUESTIONS

1. Based on Scripture, what is, in your own words, a good definition of "trust"?
2. Do you think Genesis 22 is about Abraham's faith or a picture of the cross? Why? Why not? (See Endnote 3.)
3. What promises of God have you struggled to trust in the past? How have you learned to trust God more through that experience?
4. What promise of God are you currently struggling to trust? How can Abraham's example help you?
5. Knowing that God is trustworthy, why do you think you struggle so much to trust him completely like Abraham?

ENDNOTES

1. There is much profitable discussion on how God viewed the sacrifice of Isaac. It seems from the New Testament perspective that Abraham is credited with

sacrificing Isaac even though God intervened. In other words, God viewed Abraham's actions just as if Abraham literally offered Isaac as a burnt offering rather than providing a substitute.

2. "Animal" is used because "lamb" in the ESV and other translations is a generic term concerning the flock. See Abraham Kuruvilla, *Genesis: A Theological Commentary for Preachers* (Eugene, OR: Resource Publications, 2013), 251.

3. There has been significant debate about the interpretation of this event. Jewish literature between the Testaments saw Isaac's willingness to submit to sacrifice as encouragement in martyrdom. See R.W.L. Moberly, *The Theology of the Book of Genesis* (Cambridge: Cambridge University Press, 2009), 193–196 and Jon D. Levenson, *The Death and Resurrection of the Beloved Son: The Transformation of Child Sacrifice in Judaism and Christianity* (New Haven: Yale University Press, 1993), 173–199. Other early Christian writers, along with modern writers, view this as a precursor to the cross as the father sacrifices his only son. While these views have some strength, it seems to me that, by keeping the story in its narrative context and its use in the New Testament, the focus of this chapter is on Abraham's faith and not Isaac's submission. See Kuruvilla, *Genesis*, 252.

4. This episode is a perfect parallel to the original call of Abraham in Genesis 12:1–9. For a fuller discussion and helpful chart see Kuruvilla, *Genesis*, 255, and Moberly, *The Theology of the Book of Genesis*, 186.

5. This is the first time the word "love" is used in Scripture.

6. Moriah is a significant place in Scripture as the place of sacrifice that stopped the plague in David's day (2 Sam 24:18–25) and later the site of the Temple (2 Chron 3:1). Some have argued that this incident is the foundation of the sacrificial system associated with the temple while others remain unconvinced. See Levenson, *The Death and Resurrection of the Beloved Son*, 111–124.

7. Kuruvilla, *Genesis*, 258.

8. This is the first time the word "worship" is used in Scripture. Worship is certainly present before this occasion but not the specific word (e.g., Gen 4:1–5).

9. Some believe that this had reference to the charred remains of Isaac carried by Abraham. See Levenson, *The Death and Resurrection of the Beloved Son*, 131, and others see it as a statement of trust that Isaac will live (Heb 11:17–19).

10. Kuruvilla, *Genesis*, 258.

11. Sometimes "the angel of the LORD" is thought to be the second member of the Godhead. While this is debated, it is certain that "the angel of the Lord" represents a theophany. See Tremper Longman III, *Genesis*, Story of God Bible Commentary (Grand Rapids: Zondervan, 2016), 289.

12. "'Fear of God' is the fundamental Old Testament term for depicting the appropriate human response to God—the Hebrew equivalent to the Christian 'faith.'" Kuruvilla, *Genesis*, 256. See also Moberly, *The Theology of the Book of Genesis*, 187.

13. For a fuller discussion of this see Kuruvilla, *Genesis*, 160–161, and Longman, *Genesis*, 160.

14. For a fuller discussion of Lot's presence with Abraham when he leaves for Canaan see Kuruvilla, *Genesis*, 162–163.

15. Longman, *Genesis*, 287 and Moberly, *The Theology of the Book of Genesis*, 185.

16. Josephus claims that Abraham was smarter than all others and began to believe that there was one God which caused a tumult. Josephus *A.J.* 1.154–157 (Whiston).

Chapter 5
The Last Words of Samson
Judges 16:23–31
Dewayne Tapscott

WORDS ARE POWERFUL AND LIFE-CHANGING. PEOPLE will remember our words long after we depart from this earth. How often do you remember the final words from your mother, father, sister, brother, relatives, and many other loved ones who have passed on? In Judges chapters 13–16, Samson is an emotional tragedy story rarely preached in pulpits. This is a story about a man whom God favored, who had issues with women, who could not keep his vows, and later lost his life. Samson's last recorded words were, *"Let me die with the Philistines"* (16:30 NIV). Before discussing the conclusion of his life, let us look at a few events that led up to his giving us his last words. In any physician's words regarding one's health, how did we arrive at this point?

Samson's Life

Israel did evil in the sight of the Lord, and He delivered them into the hands of the Philistines for forty years

(13:1). When Israel was in distress, the Angel appeared and instructed Manoah's wife that she would have a child. Manoah wanted to know the manner of this child's life and mission (13:11–12). Because God was fed up with Israel, He decided to raise a strong man to lead his unrepentant people out of bondage, so he hand-picked Samson's parents from the beginning. Samson, whose name signifies one that is strong and connected with the Hebrew word for 'sun' (*Shemesh*), has boundaries laid out by God as he was born a Nazarite. Endowed with prodigious strength, Samson possessed the ability to perform various remarkable exploits (e.g., slaying a lion and moving the gates of Gaza). Mark Atteberry lists in his book several descriptions of the Nazarite vow (Num 6:1–21): "(1) they had to stay away from (unwise) strong drink, (2) they had to stay away from (unclean) dead bodies, and (3) they had to stay away from the (unnecessary) cutting of the hair" (2003, 71). This vow required attention to detail, as Samson was to live under this vow for his entire life. God has instructions or principles that are to shape us into better people. Therefore, we cannot afford to ignore God's plan for our lives. Samson was physically and spiritually blessed (13:24) and lost in both (16:19–20).

Samson's Lovers

Samson had a weakness for women. His lustful eyes and the temptation of being with ungodly women brought epic failure to his life. Burton D. Fisher and Ferdinand

Lemaire noted in their book entitled *Saint-Saens's Samson and Delilah,*

> Samson acceded to his weakness and lust for pagan women by continuously visiting harlots and prostitutes —an act of blasphemy and a blatant profanation of his honor as a Nazarite and Israelite, as non-Israelite women were forbidden fruit (2004, 20).

Everyone will face temptation, but God will make a way of escape (1 Cor 10:13). If a man does not control his lust issues, then his lust issues will control him. Samson's first wife was a young Philistine woman in Timnah (she was right in his eyes) whom his parents did not approve of (14:3–5). Paraphrasing his parent's words, "Could you not find someone else?" If your godly parents with wisdom provide discernment that your friend is no good, nine out of ten times, they know what they are talking about. Samson was advised to leave the young girl alone, but his lust got in the way, he said, "Get Timnah for me." Ed Hindson pens in *Courageous Faith,* "Whenever we put pleasure ahead of principle, we are headed for trouble. It is only a matter of time before disaster strikes" (2003, 124). As God was with him even though he made terrible relationship choices, He killed a lion with his bare hands (14:6). He scraped the lion's carcass, ate of it, and told the Philistines a riddle for them to figure out. His wife pressed the issue until she got the answer from him and told her people. As with any marriage with problems, Samson left to cool off, then decided to go home and be with his wife. However, her father thought he was so angry with her that he decided to give her over to Samson's best man (a friend who was guarding him) (14:20–15:6). Once again, due to his anger issues, the Philistines burned Samson's wife and her father.

In chapter sixteen (16:1–3), Samson's lust tempted him to be with a harlot. Based on evidence from scripture, we can see how long that relationship lasted. One verse later (16:4), he was now in love with Delilah. This temptation was the ultimate fall. Samson was falling in love with these women without consulting God about it. He was failing at relationships because he refused wise counsel from his parents (Prov 13:1, 15:5). Delilah exploited Samson's trust and vulnerability. She asked him numerous times what his weakness was, and he continued to give her false information. After Delilah managed to seduce the secrets of his strength, she then lulled Samson to sleep on her lap, and cut seven locks of his hair (16:19). There was nothing magical about his hair, as it was the symbol of his consecration to God. The Devil will agitate you until he breaks you (Jas 4:7). Ed Hindson also mentions six practical steps when dealing with temptation: "(1) Take a good look at yourself, (2) Admit you have a problem, (3) Believe that God can make a difference in your life, (4) Make a total commitment, (5) Renewal is a full-time job, and (6) Take the "way of escape!" (2003, 133).

Samson's Legacy

Samson's sins cost him (Num 32:23). The vow had been broken, and he could not free himself. Samson was now in prison, and the woman he loved was not thinking of him at all. The enemy will mess with your mind, head, and heart, and cause you to sleep before destroying you. Samson lost touch with God. I often wonder how many lost touch with God during the pandemic. Here is a man who had it all, lost it all, and now he had some final words to say. Samson would soon learn that restoration is just a prayer away. Wendell Winkler mentions Samson's issues in *Samon's Sins*: "He was self-willed, obstinate, rebellious, refused the wise counsel of his parents, chose evil associations and therefore became disloyal to his vow" (1973, 8–13). Samson, with a vexed soul as a prisoner, was now flirting with a death wish. He was now blind, in chains, and was called to the temple to entertain the crowd. At the end of his life, Samson was trying to rewrite the past. James Crenshaw notes in *Samson* how a man's death wish appears different in biblical literature:

(1) someone who finds himself in desperate straits;—(2) she or he requests death from God;—(3) reasons with the person asking to die;—(4) he or she chooses to continue living;—(5) a fifth motif is due to a loss of charisma which delineates its characteristics (1978, 46–48).

When Samson asked Yahweh to remember the promise given to his parents (16:28), he asked Yahweh to remember his Nazarite relationship. Paul K.-K. Cho expressed in *Willingness To Die and The Gift of Life* that

Samson obeyed the Philistine command to provide entertainment to pursue his own volitional end. Samson then proceeds to carry out his attack, which was the final cause for changing his mind about the Philistines' absurd commands (2020, 92).

Samson prayed his last prayer as they wanted to make a sport of him. The crowd was praising their god (Dagon), saying their god was stronger than the God of Israel because they had conquered Samson. He was willing to die because he had the will to kill three thousand people. With the restoration of his hair, he stood between two pillars of Dagon's temple, which were holding up the building, and found his vengeful retribution, causing the roof to collapse. Samson killed more at his death than he did when he was alive.

Closing Thought

Samson (1)allowed women to upset him so much that he forgot his mission; (2) he failed to analyze his anger as his anger hindered him, and (3) instead of focusing on God's mission, he focused on his sins that cost him very dearly. Sin blinds you; it enslaves you (John 8:34), weakens you (1 Cor 11:30), and divides you from God (Isa 59:1–2), as sin brings death (Ezek. 18:20 and Rom 6:23). Samson gave us a glimpse of a dying man's legacy! He lost his vision and vitality and forfeited his fellowship and freedom. We sometimes fail and may even want to give up (Isa 40:29–31), but God will give us strength if we trust in Him (Rom 12:19). Samson was shackled by sin and shamed by sin. During the 1950s, NAACP leaders Nyasha Junior and Jeremy Schipper penned an interesting quote in *Black Samson*,

We must be like blind Samson, willing to pull away the pillars of authority and bring down the whole temple of greed and corruption that would hitch us to the treadmill of inferiority and degradation (2020, 67).

Discussion Questions: Samson vs. Us Today?

1. Discuss weaknesses that Samson faced that Christians might be facing now.
2. Discuss the dangers of a broken "vow" in the Old Testament.
3. Talk about the comment made: Our "god" hath delivered into our hands our enemy, and the destroyer of our country which slew many of us (16:24).
4. Discuss the Temple of Dagon (16:25) and why Samson sacrificed his life to take the lives of others.
5. What makes us so angry that we become destructive? (Eph 4:26).

Bibliography

Attebury, Mark. *The Samson Syndrome*. Nashville: Thomas Nelson, 2003.

Cho, Paul K.-K. *Willingness To Die and The Gift of Life*. Eerdmans, 2020.

Crenshaw, James L. *Samson*. Atlanta: John Knox Press, 1978.

Fisher, Burton D. and Ferdinand Lemaire. *Saint-

Saens: Samson and Delilah. s.l.: Opera Journeys Publishing, 2004.

Hindson, Ed. *Courageous Faith.* Chattanooga, TN: AMG Publishers, 2003.

Junior, Nyasha, and Jeremy Schipper. *Black Samson.* New York: Oxford University Press, 2020.

Winkler, Wendell. *Samson's Sins: And Other Sermons.* Fort Worth, TX: Winkler Publications, 1973.

Chapter 6
Persevering Under Pressure!
Job 1
Mark Posey

TEXT

Job 1:1–21

Introduction

Job is a character from the Bible, as confirmed in Ezekiel 14:14 and James 5:11. Despite the challenges, he remained loyal to God, showing unwavering commitment to doing good. Valuable lessons are learned from his perseverance and faith.

Life Lessons We Will Learn

- Bad things happen to good people.
- We must hold steadfast to our hope in God.
- God's way is the only right way.

Discussion

Notice a contextual study of Job 1:1–21.

1. **Job 1:1**

a. Job lived in the "land of Uz;" his name means "hated."

b. Job's character is described with a quartet of qualities (cf., 1:8, 2:3): **Blameless** (Job could not be justly charged with moral failure), **Upright** (Job lived life with his head held high, not in arrogance), **Feared God** (Job respected and revered God), and **Shunned Evil** (Job kept his distance from that which was wrong).

2. **Job 1:2**

a. Large families are uncommon in our current culture, but they were typical in the past, especially during the patriarchs' reign.

b. The number 10 in biblical literature is a completed course of time or completeness in divine order. Job had seven sons and three daughters.

3. **Job 1:3**

a. Job's financial portfolio was extensive. In the ancient world, possessions determined a man's status in society. Job was a man of impressive wealth and status.

b. East in the first five books of the Old Testament was more principle-related than directional. When people moved east, they moved away from God.

c. In the East, there was a prime example of moral goodness. His name was Job—he was the greatest of all the men of the East.

4. **Job 1:4**

45

a. Job's family was typical. They gathered "on his appointed day."

b. In Hebrew, "his appointed day" implies a birthday. Thus, their family, like many of ours, would celebrate each family member's birthday.

5. **Job 1:5**

a. Job took his duties as the patriarch of his family very seriously: he moved with urgency (e.g., "he would rise early in the morning") and consistency (e.g., "Thus Job did regularly" [continually—NASB]).

b. Job's concern for his children is seen in this verse: "For Job said, 'It may be that my sons have sinned and cursed God in their hearts.'" Job's fear was justifiable. The words "sinned" and "cursed" are emphatic. The term "cursed" (i.e., originally *chalal*, but replaced with *barach*) means "to abandon, leave, blaspheme, turn away." Job was concerned that his children had left God. Thus, he focused on their spiritual well-being.

6. **Job 1:6**

a. One day, the "sons of God" (commonly associated with angels. Cf. Gen 6:1–4) met with God.

b. This meeting seemed private, but Satan showed up uninvited and unannounced. The phrase "also came among them" in Hebrew indicates that one is present but uninvited.

7. **Job 1:7**

a. The dialogue between the Lord and Satan is fascinating. Satan was asked about his activities (c.f., 1 Pet 5:8). The Devil wanted to "devour," meaning "to drink down, swallow up, destroy, rip, shred, tear, mutilate." Our encounter with the Devil happens on a battleground, where he seeks to destroy everything.

8.**Job 1:8**

a. The Lord presented Satan with a test subject. Notice the close fellowship between the Lord and Job: "my"—possessive pronoun; "servant"—Hebrew (*ebed*)—slave, manservant, worshipper; "there is none like him on the earth"—Job held a special status. Cf. 1:1, 8; 2:3.

b. The Lord's estimation of Job was exceedingly high and full of confidence.

9.**Job 1:9**

a. Here, Satan fulfilled the role described in Revelation 12:10—*the accuser of the brethren.* Satan accused Job before God, insisting that Job's godliness was false and that he only served God for what he could get from Him.

b. Satan is a deceiver (2 Cor 11:14, John 8:44), tempter (Matt 4:3, 1 Thess 3:5), thief (John 10:10), murderer (John 8:44), and distorter (Gen 3:5).

c. We must follow James's admonition: "Resist the devil, and he will flee from you" (Jas 4:7).

10.**Job 1:10**

a. Satan's accusations were bold but true. We are fortunate to receive every blessing and act of protection from God. Cf. Luke 22:31–32.

b. Job was strong, blessed, wealthy, healthy, and respected. The Lord had blessed him exceedingly.

11.**Job 1:11**

a. Satan levied a challenge! I.e., If you damage all his property and possessions, he will "curse" You without hesitation. Cf. Job 1:5.

b. Satan's challenge: Withhold Your blessings and

protection, and You will see Job move from faith to rebellion, strength to failure, and dependence to rejection.

12.**Job 1:12**

a. In response to Satan's accusation, God permitted him to attack Job. God would let down the *hedge* without completely removing it; however, God remained in control.

b. Thus, Satan went to work to prove his premise (i.e., Job's noble motive in serving God was false). Thus, if Job was faking, everyone else was likely to do the same!

c. Satan's challenge had to be met! Job was in the perfect position to silence Satan's false accusations.

13.**Job 1:13–15**

a. Notice the phrase "a day." The Hebrew word for "day" is *yowm*. It depicts a 24-hour period. Thus, the following events unfolded in Job's life due to the actions of Satan, all occurring in a single day.

b. **Catastrophe #1**—The oxen and donkeys were stolen, servants viciously murdered, and only one escaped to bring the bad news to Job.

i. Satan used evil people to carry out his attack.

ii. The Sabeans were an ancient people mentioned in the Bible as coming from a nation far away from Israel (Joel 3:8). They were a people of stature (Isa 45:14) and a rival nation to Israel (Job 1:15). The Sabeans lived in the land of Sheba, which archeology suggests was a Semitic trading state that existed for 1,000 years in the area that is now Yemen.

14.**Job 1:16**

a. The first messenger had not finished his horror tale

when the second messenger arrived with a story of the destruction of greater magnitude.

b. **Catastrophe #2**—The sheep were grazing, and the shepherds [servants] were watching. Suddenly, a violent storm arose, and lightning [fire of God] struck and killed 7,000 sheep (1:3) and many servants.

i. The words "fire" and "consumed" are the same as those in 1 Kings 18:38 on Mount Carmel. Elijah cried to God, and fire rained down from above.

ii. God's fire consumed Job's sheep and servants. The severity of such an occurrence is likely unparalleled in our modern context. In 1 Kings 18, God sent fire to prove His power over the false prophets and their fictitious deities; however, in Job 1, Satan was the force behind the fire that destroyed Job's livestock and servants. The "fire of God" was lightning.

iii. Only one servant escaped with his life to be the bearer of horrific news.

15. **Job 1:17**

a. **Catastrophe #3**—The Chaldeans demonstrated military training, i.e., "formed three bands," two flanking and one frontal assault: 3,000 camels were stolen, and many servants were murdered.

b. Only one servant escaped with his life to be the bearer of horrific news.

16. **Job 1:18–19**

a. A family gathering quickly came to a tragic end. This is the worst of Job's losses.

b. **Catastrophe #4**—While festively enjoying family time, Job's children were unaware of Satan's plans.

Suddenly, a wilderness wind forced the collapse of the oldest brother's house, killing all 10 of Job's children.

c. Job's animals, servants, and children all perished because Job was the target of unimaginable evil. The loss of his children was the most severe of all the calamities Satan brought.

d. Losing a child is one of the—if not the—most difficult tragedies to experience. However, I have often wondered, would the loss of three children be three times as difficult, or the loss of seven be seven times more severe? What if you lost ten children simultaneously? Who knows the pain one would be forced to endure under such adversity?

e. Only one servant escaped with his life to be the bearer of horrific news.

f. **Questions:** Having lost so much, what would a person do? What would a person say? In this case, we do not have to guess; we are told in verses 20 and 21.

17. **Job 1:20**

a. First, Job arose. He did not remain stagnant; he kept moving.

b. Second, Job tore his robe; he ripped his clothes. Fashion should not be our greatest concern in times of significant loss and terrible heartache.

c. Third, Job shaved his head. My hair is the least of my concerns when such a tragedy occurs.

d. Fourth, Job fell to the ground. He lost strength in all parts of his body.

e. Fifth, Job went to the Lord. Job went to the right source for help!

18. **Job 1:21**

a. First, Job spoke of birth. We bring nothing with us when we enter this world, Job observed. Cf. 1 Timothy 6:7a.

b. Second, Job spoke of death. He identified that we will take nothing when we leave this world—Cf. 1 Timothy 6:7b.

c. NOTE: Job set critical parameters; the period between birth and death. We call that period LIFE! That's where each of us is right now—we're in the middle of LIFE!

d. Third, Job spoke of divine ownership. Everything belongs to God; what we have is on loan from Him. Cf. Psalm 24:1.

e. Fourth, Job spoke of loss. Since God owns everything, doesn't He have the right to take away what He has given us at any time and for any reason?

f. Fifth, Job spoke of praise. God is the source of all that is good. We receive good and perfect gifts from Him. Praise be to God!

19.**Job 1:22**

a. In this passage, Job's moral character is highlighted as he refrained from sinning or wrongly blaming God.

b. Job did not turn his back on God despite tremendous pressure and severe trials. Job silenced Satan's accusation and proved God's way is the only right way!

Conclusion

Job provides a beautiful demonstration of Perseverance Under Pressure! He remained faithful to God under the direst of circumstances. Thank God for Job's example and influence!

Discussion Questions

1. What qualities in Job's character do you find most admirable? Why?
2. How can Job's response to his losses serve as a guiding example for overcoming trials in your own life?
3. How does the story of Job challenge the prosperity gospel's idea that earthly success is a sign of God's favor?
4. How can you incorporate Job's principle of integrity into your personal, professional, or spiritual life?
5. After studying Job 1:1–22, what is your understanding of why bad things happen to good people?
6. How does the Book of Job, Chapter 1, prompt you to reconsider your perception of blessings?

Chapter 7
God's Faithfulness
Psalm 89
Thomas Tidwell

I thank my God always when I remember you in my prayers, because I hear of your love and of the faith that you have toward the Lord Jesus and for all the saints, and I pray that the sharing of your faith may become effective for the full knowledge of every good thing that is in us for the sake of Christ. For I have derived much joy and comfort from your love, my brother, because the hearts of the saints have been refreshed through you Philemon 1:4–7. (All quotes in this chapter will come from the English Standard Version of the Bible.)

WHAT A BEAUTIFUL THOUGHT FOR A CHAPTER IN A great series of studies known as the Onesimus Bible Study Series.

The church today needs to be refreshed. It needs hope. It needs to know that God is still on His throne and is looking out for His people as He did in the Old Testament. We need to be reminded of the promise made by our Savior when He said in Matthew 28:20, "... *And behold, I am with you always, to the end of the age."* What comfort! What love, what passion for the people of the world, in His willingness to die for us.

In the Old Testament, we see God encouraging His people time and again. He wants them to know and trust that He is there to aid them. He lets them know that, though they sin, there is mercy and grace from God. One of the greatest passages that brings comfort, yet also discusses the reality of brokenness because of sin, is Psalm 89. This psalm is attributed to Ethan the Ezrahite, and he starts off praising the steadfast love of the Lord. As we stop to consider this first verse, Ethan wants all to know that God is a God who keeps His promises. He teaches and preaches God's faithfulness—what a glorious thought! In a world where people make so many promises but fail to keep them, we can always know that when God speaks, He will do as He says.

Ethan discusses the covenant that God made with David.

> *I have made a covenant with my chosen one; I have sworn to David my servant: I will establish your offspring forever and build your throne for all generations* (Psa 89:3–4).

We know the reference to David's offspring indicates Jesus's coming and saving mankind. Jesus's willingness to die on the cross for mankind showed His complete trust in the plan of the Godhead to save mankind. When Jesus died on the cross and was buried, many thought it was the end. Many today, sadly, are not aware of what the

Father, the Son, and the Spirit have done to save man from their sins. David's offspring are the descendants of David through Christ—of which we have a part because we have been baptized into Christ. What a privilege to be of "royal seed" because we have been saved by Jesus's blood and have been baptized "into him" (Rom 6:3–4).

God's faithfulness to His promises is a great source of joy. Ethan emphasizes that God is "greatly to be feared and awesome among those who are around him." (Psa 89:8). Consider that we have lost the fear of God in our country and in the world. We do not seek His will, we fail in our sins and shortcomings of His commands, and we lose our faith and walk away. Statistics today concerning the church should break all our hearts as we consider how we are losing so many of our young people. Closing church doors permanently because no one comes should break our hearts. God is faithful to us—are we to Him? Please consider, as well, that as God is faithful to His promises, He expects the same out of us.

Psalm 89:9–18 reminds us of God's power! He is the one who rules the raging of the sea, and He is the one who stills the waves. He oversees the heavens, the earth, and the world because He has created them all (Psa 89:11).

Further, "righteousness and justice are the foundation of your throne" (Psa 89:14). God will always do what is right. Our lives will be judged by how we live. Are we prepared for the reality of judgment? Do we live daily, striving to obey His commands? Have we sought righteousness and justice in our daily lives? When God's people know God; when they worship God in the ways

He has specified, they know that God would be pleased with them. We need to work on our relationships with God and on our worship of Him. In any given worship service of the Lord, we have those who have come to worship Him in every way they can. But some get easily distracted by babies, by an "off-key song," by a mispronunciation of a Bible passage, or by a gaffe in a prayer. Satan is doing all he can to keep God's children from worshipping Him "in spirit and in truth."

God makes promises to David in Psalm 89:21–37 via Nathan the prophet. As we study this, consider the fact that Jesus is a descendant of David (Matt 1:6–16), and this passage denotes a dual fulfillment—first through David the king, then through David's seed, Jesus. Notice that God promises to strengthen Him, and no enemy will outwit Him. We see Jesus being tempted by Satan in Matthew 4:1–11, and Jesus defeated Satan in all his attempts. He has shown us that we, too, can defeat Satan if we are wise to his devices (2 Cor 2:11).

Notice some of the parallels between David and Jesus. Jesus and David were both kings, with Jesus being King of kings and Lord of lords (Rev 19:16). God was with David to strengthen him (Psa 89:21). In Luke 22:43 an angel was sent to Jesus to strengthen Him. David was given divine assistance in his kingdom, and so is Jesus.

David, as well as Jesus, cried out, "You are my Father, My God and the rock of my salvation." (Psa 89:26). Jesus cried out, "My God, My God why have You forsaken Me?" (Matt 27:46)

David fought many battles as a king, and Jesus fought many battles against those who opposed Him. David won most of his battles, and Jesus won over the deceit that Satan tried to stop Him from the cross.

In Psalm 89:26 we find David saying, "You are my Father, My God and the Rock of my salvation." How often did Jesus refer to the Father in His ministry? According to one source, over 165 times. David, as well as Jesus, had a great relationship with God. Both would cry out to Him, and David and his seed would prosper forever.

In Psalm 89:29–33, we are told that the throne and seed of David would endure as long as the world stands. While his children may forsake the law (v 30) and be punished, God will not remove them from "my steadfast love, or be false to His faithfulness." In this, we see God's patience with His people—indeed, His patience with all people. We see that He will punish their iniquities and transgressions, ". . . *But I will* NOT *remove from him my steadfast love or be false to my faithfulness.*" God will love man, even if man does not reciprocate that love. God does not violate the covenant, nor can He violate who He is. Hence David's offspring, Jesus, shall endure as long as the sun is before Him. The sun and the moon are faithful witnesses to the promises of God—but we are again reminded that one day all this will be destroyed.

In Psalm 89:38–45, we see a prophecy of the crucifixion of Jesus. Jesus, even as King of kings and Lord of lords, paid the ultimate price for us to be saved. He was "cast off and rejected", and God was ". . . full of wrath against your anointed." The chief priests mocked Him (Mark 15:27). Peter denied Him (Matt 27:69). The soldiers mocked Jesus (Matt 27:27–31) as the King of kings, the Lord of lords, was on the cross (Matt 27:32–37), dying for our sins.

God watched His Son die on the cross. Those six hours must have been filled with excruciating pain. The psalmist asks, "How long will your wrath burn like fire?" We cannot even begin to know the pain Jesus endured on the cross, lifting Himself on the nails in His feet and hands.

Finally, we see the cry, "How long, O Lord, will you hide yourself forever? How long will your wrath burn like fire?" Remember how short My time is! Jesus's time on earth was a short period, but consider how He must have felt on the cross during those six hours!

David must have understood much of this, as he "... bears in my heart the insults of many nations, with which your enemies mock, O Lord ..." (39:50).

Our lives here on earth are short. Our faith on earth is either built by steadfast commitment to God or diminished when we try to do things our way rather than God's.

What we believe about God impacts the rest of our lives. The Psalmist in the passage above emphasizes that we must have a relationship with God, when it seems like He is there, or when it seems like He is not. He loves us! He gets us! He wants us with Him. May we honor Him with our lips, as well as our entire lives.

Some of this has been borrowed from *WISDOM LITERATURE AND PSALMS*, James Smith via Logos.

Discussion Questions

1. In what ways does strong confidence in God's faithfulness bless us?
2. In what ways does the devil tempt us to question God's faithfulness?
3. Why did God—who owes no one anything—choose to make and record amazing promises to Abraham, David, and us?
4. How does comparing Jesus to David call us to stronger faith?
5. How can we best deal with the "tension" between our knowledge of God's faithfulness and our frequent desire for God to act like we think He should act?

Chapter 8
Proverbs 1:1–7
Lucas Suddreth

Focus Passage

Prov 1:1–7 (ESV)

>"The proverbs of Solomon, son of David, king of Israel:
>To know wisdom and instruction,
>to understand words of insight,
>to receive instruction in wise dealing,
>in righteousness, justice, and equity;
>to give prudence to the simple,
>knowledge and discretion to the youth—
>Let the wise hear and increase in learning,
>and the one who understands obtain guidance,
>to understand a proverb and a saying,
>the words of the wise and their riddles.
>The fear of the LORD is the beginning of knowledge;
>fools despise wisdom and instruction."

Introduction

The first nine chapters of Proverbs serve as a manual on how to gain wisdom. Solomon addresses his son, emphasizing the importance of wisdom for a man of God, especially a king. He contrasts the destructive path of foolishness with the life-giving way of wisdom. However, comparing wisdom with the way of the world is not very attention-grabbing. Solomon recognizes that his son understands the reasons to pursue wisdom, yet he still worries that it's not enough to convince him. Solomon knows the mind of a young man is easily distracted by the world, so he describes wisdom in a way that would be incredibly appealing to a young man—a potential love interest. For example, in Proverbs 3:15–18, Solomon describes wisdom as a beautiful lady who can grant long life, riches, and honor. While modern readers might bristle at the way Solomon encourages his son to "lay hold of her [Lady Wisdom]" (3:18), he cleverly attempts to associate two desirable things—his son's natural desire for romance and the desire for knowledge and understanding (or wisdom). Together, they will grant his son a happy and fulfilled life.

Despite Solomon's son, Rehoboam, failing to wholeheartedly seek the Lord (2 Chron 12:14), Solomon was still successful in his efforts. At the very least, his words were recorded so men and women across the ages might hear and learn from them. In fact, scholars suggest that Solomon wasn't only addressing his son, he was writing for the benefit of everyone. He is hoping that we, the readers, will listen to his words, seek after wisdom, and cultivate a lifelong relationship with her. With this in mind, let's explore exactly what Solomon has to say to the ancient reader and us today!

Going Deeper

> Prov 1:1 *The proverbs of Solomon, son of David, king of Israel:*
>> Prov 1:2 *To know wisdom and instruction,*
>> *to understand words of insight,*
>> Prov 1:3 *to receive instruction in wise dealing,*
>> *in righteousness, justice, and equity.*

Solomon begins by highlighting the benefits of reading and responding positively toward the Proverbs. In the second verse, he asserts that they will help the reader *to know wisdom*. This means they will not only know (or recognize) wisdom, but will also learn, and internalize, its teachings. By doing so, wisdom becomes their teacher, instructing and correcting them in the ways of wisdom (v. 3).

Verse three emphasizes the importance of taking this teaching and correction to heart because wisdom will impart the fundamental values of being a good human being. Righteousness, justice, and equity are essential values for God's followers because they foster a love for one's neighbor. These values promote peace and harmony and serve as the bedrock for a thriving society.

Michael V. Fox describes these three characteristics in this way:

- Righteousness "is the principle of right behavior and justice ... in word and deed."
- Justice "is the right and just condition ... the right state of affairs or the right mode of behavior."
- Equity "means straightness and levelness ... Most often [it] indicates the quality or result of honest, fair speech or judgment."[1]

In simpler terms, righteousness is our desire for upright speech and actions; justice is our desire to see righteous action within our world; and equity means we want to see both righteousness and justice applied uniformly to all.

It's worth noting that these three words—righteousness, justice, and equity—overlap slightly in their definitions. This overlap emphasizes the necessity for followers of God to treat all people fairly in both word and deed. Solomon explains it to the reader using these three different words. While these words are often thrown around in political circles today, long before this, they were used to describe those who allowed the wisdom in Proverbs to teach and correct them in treating all people fairly.

Prov 1:4 *to give prudence to the simple,*
knowledge and discretion to the youth—
Prov 1:5 *Let the wise hear and increase in learning,*

and the one who understands obtain guidance,
Prov 1:6 *to understand a proverb and a saying,*
the words of the wise and their riddles.

Having thoroughly explained the benefits of the
Proverbs and their importance, Solomon now describes
the two groups who would benefit most from these
words: the simple and the wise. While we don't often use
the adjective "simple" to describe ourselves or others,
Solomon employs it here to refer to the young and naïve.
Rather than being derogatory, he is speaking of those who
are discerning what it means to live a good life and be a
good person. The individuals who are, most often the
young who stand at the threshold of adulthood, are faced
with the decision of either following wisdom or foolishness. Solomon's hope is that the simple, young, and naïve
will leave their current state and grow into maturity,
embracing a life filled with wisdom.

Many of us can recall this stage of our lives—being
young and naïve, and trying to figure out how to be a
well-functioning human. I'm sure we all have stories of
the mistakes we made along the way, but thankfully,
many of us have matured enough to embrace wisdom.

While it makes perfect sense that the young, simple,
and naïve would benefit from hearing these words, the
second group to benefit is the wise (1:5). To most of us,
this may seem ironic, but the point is that the wise are
always learning and growing. They recognize that being
in a relationship with lady wisdom takes effort and
commitment!

Even Solomon with all his wisdom struggled to maintain his relationship with wisdom. Later in his life, he built high places for his wives and concubines to worship foreign gods (1 Kgs 11:1–8). This was obviously an act of foolishness, and I believe the reason was that he had neglected his relationship with wisdom. It had taken a back seat in his life, falling down his list of priorities. As a result, he made mistakes that led him away from wisdom and God.

This is why Solomon addresses the wise in his introduction to Proverbs. It is because they will spend the rest of their lives learning from and growing in wisdom. Only a fool would think they have mastered it.

Prov 1:7 *The fear of the LORD is the beginning of knowledge; fools despise wisdom and instruction.*

With verse seven, we now reach the climax of our text and the motto of the entire book. Solomon asserts that whether one is young and simple or old and wise, the path to wisdom begins with fearing the Lord.

Over the years, the phrase "fear of the Lord" has been interpreted in various ways leading to some confusion. However, a helpful analogy is to compare it to the relationship between a child and their father. While parenting styles vary, for many of us, our fathers played the role of disciplinarian. They were the ones we feared after we were caught acting out. Most of us would say we respected and loved our fathers, yet simultaneously feared their discipline, disapproval, and punishment.

In the same way, we are to fear God. This doesn't mean we cower before Him; rather, we bow in awe of His power and majesty. We are concerned at His disapproval and worry about His punishment. But, the fear of God should mature beyond mere worry or concern. It should develop into a respect for God that arises from understanding and knowledge of Him. Again, it is similar to our relationship with our earthly father. As children, we fear our fathers' discipline, but as we mature, we hopefully come to respect him because we comprehend him better. We understand that our fathers intended to teach us and shape us into well-functioning human beings. This is similar to how we approach God. As our relationship with Him matures, we understand that He is molding us into individuals characterized by righteousness, justice, and equity (1:1–3).

Application

Having read through the text, it's clear that Solomon is calling us to do three things:

1. **Seek wisdom.** Solomon calls the simple to leave their naïve state and reminds the wise that a relationship with wisdom takes continuous effort. This message applies to us today because we all fall into one of these two categories, and the challenge is to properly discern which category we are in. The most important question to answer is *are we spending time seeking after the wisdom of God?* If not, then we may be closer to the simple and naïve.

2. **Know wisdom.** Going beyond mere recognition or factual understanding, we are called to know, learn, and internalize the teachings of wisdom: righteousness, justice, and equity. A great way to discern how well we

know wisdom is to ask ourselves: *Is Biblical righteousness, justice, and equity a significant part of my life?*

3. **Submit to the Lord.** When Solomon speaks of fearing the Lord, he is addressing the attitude we should have toward Him—an attitude of submission and acknowledgment that God is trying to teach us and shape us into well-functioning human beings. The critical question for us is, *do we submit and allow Him to teach and mold us?* In a society that holds freedom and independence as cardinal virtues, this submission remains vitally important.

Conclusion

Having examined Solmon's words, it's clear that he is calling the young, the wise, and everyone in between to read the book of Proverbs. By doing so they can know, learn, and possess wisdom. This is vital for God's children because the characteristics of wisdom—righteousness, justice, and equity—are fundamental values for God's people.

The first step for us all is submission to the will of God. Only then can we genuinely seek wisdom and come to know it.

Discussion Questions

1. Is godly wisdom properly valued by most people today? Why?

2. Why is the guidance of Scripture essential in identifying godly wisdom?
3. What are the major differences between godly wisdom and worldly wisdom?
4. What is the relationship between true wisdom and humility? Lifelong learning?

Endnotes

[1] Michael V. Fox, *Proverbs 1–9*, The Anchor Yale Bible; (New Haven: Yale University Press, 1974), 60.

Chapter 9
Come Now, Let Us Reason Together
Isaiah 1:18
Walter Rayburn

God's Call to Engage Our Minds

IN OUR SOCIETY, THE ABILITY TO CRITICALLY examine an idea and logically defend one's position is becoming a rarity. Often, people will rely on emotions to uphold their positions rather than having rational conversations with those with whom they have disagreements. One only has to turn on political talk shows, watch the local news coverage of one of the seemingly endless protests in our nation, or scroll through a social media entertainment site to discover people passionately defending their opinion or viciously attacking those who disagree with them. They do this with absolutely no basis in logic or reason. Unfortunately, this type of behavior found its way into our religious discussions in the last generation. When people discuss religious beliefs or moral standards in our world, they often believe that those who demonstrate the most anger, sadness, or exuberance must be the ones who are accurately handling the Word of God. Knowledge and reason often take a backseat to zeal to the detriment of all involved. Many people living in our society insist that Jesus brought us a religion of emotion which left the mind out of the equation. For this reason, God's words in **Isaiah 1:18** have become one of my favorite passages from the Old Testament and guidance that I find myself relying on more and more. They encourage us to resist the pressures of the world which tell us to abandon knowledge of the truth for the pacification found in human emotions. Let us now consider the words of this great prophet.

God Opens the Lines of Communication

God begins addressing Isaiah with the simple words, *"Come now, and let us reason together"* (Isa 1:18a). Due to multiple possible definitions of the Hebrew word translated as "reason", the exact meaning of this passage is somewhat up for debate.[1] However, all the options presented to us include one basic idea: God calls us to engage our minds with open dialogue and critical thought of His Words if we wish to fully understand His nature and His plans for our future! In other words, God wants to have a genuine conversation with us about His intentions for us. While it would be easy to take this idea for granted, we need to peel back the layers of what this truly means for us.

First, it means that God wants to speak to us. Again, it is easy to take this for granted, but it is a truly amazing thing that the Creator of the world and all that is in it desires to speak to us. He longs to spread His wisdom to

His creation. He has worked to both prepare and protect His written word in order to deliver to mankind a message of salvation and hope to counter the darkness of the world. He confidently promises us that *"The Word of the Lord endures forever"* (1 Pet 1:25). The love that powers this desire to communicate with us is immeasurable and must be revered.

Second, it means that God has lowered Himself to communicate with His creation. God makes it clear that we are infinitely inferior to Him in all ways. *"For as the heavens are higher than the earth, so are My ways higher than your ways, and My thoughts than your thoughts"* (Isa 55:9). He will even go so far as to describe the greatest wisdom of this world as nothing but foolishness when compared to His immense wisdom (1 Cor 1:20). Despite this fact, God chooses to pass on His infinite wisdom to us like a father handing earthly wisdom to a toddler who is completely ignorant of the world that surrounds him. We must never fail to appreciate that our God chooses not only to speak to us but to speak to us in such a way that we can both understand and obey Him.

Third, it means that we have an obligation to God to consider all that He has to tell us. If our omnipotent, omniscient, omnipresent, and omnibenevolent God puts forth the effort to open the line of communication with us, we must put forth the effort to both learn and understand all that He has to say to us. The ball is truly in our court. God has given us all the knowledge we need to survive this world and reach our eternal home.

*All scripture is inspired by God and profitable for teach-
ing, for reproof, for correction, for training in righteousness; so that the man of God may be adequate,
equipped for every good work* (2 Tim 3:16–17).

What will we do with this great and wonderful gift?
If we choose to be servants of God, we must devote time,
effort, energy, and resources to learn all that we can from
our God. *"Be diligent to present yourself approved to God
as a workman who does not need to be ashamed, accurately handling the word of truth"* (2 Tim 2:16). Only by
engaging our mind can we possibly do all that God asks
us to do with His Word.

The Reward for Reasoning with God

As is so often the case, God does not give us a task
without also revealing the reward for fulfilling the task.
*"Though your sins are as scarlet, they will be as white as
snow; though they are red like crimson, they will be like
wool"* (Isa 1:18b). God makes a beautiful promise to
those who devote effort to consider His Word with an
open and sincere heart. Their sins, regardless of the
number or the severity, will be washed away and forgiven
completely by His infinite grace and mercy.

The life of sin leaves its mark on the soul. When
James described the beautiful religion of God, he
included the idea that we must remain unspotted by the
world that surrounds us (Jas 1:27). When we give in to
sin, the stains that are left behind accumulate on our
souls. As God speaks with Isaiah, He sees the soul as so

completely covered in these stains that they appear to be solid red when they were once white with innocence and purity. In that moment, God offers salvation to the one who will consider His Word. He will cleanse their stains and restore the innocent state of the obedient. With such a great and wonderful promise on the table, we must ask how all this works!

First, we must understand that, if a person truly considers what God has said in His Word, he or she will choose to obey God. Faith is not a blind leap. Rather, it is a measured and reasonable conclusion one will arrive at when considering all the evidence. The beginning of reasoning with God is coming to a belief in God based on the evidence He has left behind.

> For since the creation of the world His invisible attributes, His eternal power and divine nature, have been clearly seen, being understood through what has been made, so that they are without excuse (Rom 1:20).

Once a person arrives at a basic belief in a god, he or she will consider the Bible in order to find the true God of Heaven. The Word of God is incomparable and demonstrates itself as trustworthy and reliable. Again, God is happy to meet us as we discuss the reliability of His Word. He will offer His evidence, which overwhelmingly leads us to the conclusion that it is the inerrant, inspired Word of Jehovah.

Once a person concludes that the Bible is God's Word, he or she will investigate it to discover the wisdom God has revealed. As noted above, this is the basic duty of man in response to God's Word. If we truly believe that an all-knowing being has chosen to give us information, what could possibly keep us from devoting time to gaining that information? I once heard a lesson that described ways Christians can demonstrate their atheism. I cannot think of a more apt example of this than a person who claims to believe in God but refuses to spend time learning from Him through Bible study!

After investigating the Word of God to discover its beautiful message, a reasonable person will obey God. If a person has found the God of the Bible to be true, why would he or she refuse to yield? If a person has a problem with their car and takes it to a mechanic who offers a solution to the problem at a reasonable price with a 100% guarantee, the person would be illogical to not accept the offer! When a person learns of their sin problem and comes to God who offers a foolproof solution as a reward for obedience, that person would have to be insane or driven by biased human emotions to reject the offer.

It is here that the Word of God fulfills its ultimate purpose. When a person is led first by the mind to find the true God of this earth, the heart will quickly join in order to lead a person to full obedience and salvation. The KNOWLEDGE of God and His Son will naturally lead us to the EMOTION of a heartfelt relationship with Jehovah. The greatest lesson I believe we can learn from God's invitation to reason together is that we must put the mind first in order to understand God so that we can have a genuine emotional response to His overwhelming love for us.

Discussion Questions

1. List some practical ways to truly investigate the word of God on a deep level.
2. What are some ways we see people's hearts overruling their minds in the religious world?
3. Discuss the connection between the mind and the heart in the life of a Christian.
4. What are some of the applications we can discover from Isaiah 1:18?
5. What is the natural result when a person truly comes together to reason with God?

Endnote

[1] Homer Hailey, *A Commentary On Isaiah* (Grand Rapids: Baker Books, 1985), 41–42.

Chapter 10
A Lasting Promise
Isaiah 43:2–3
Ralph Richardson

Focus Passage

Isaiah 43:2–3

One Main Thing

Some people allow the circumstances of their lives to separate them from God. No one is immune from being exposed to the temptations and tragedies of life that can—and often do—occur. While we may not have a choice as to the calamities that appear in our lives, we do not have to navigate these uncertainties alone. God has a fixed presence in the life of His children, and it is up to us to decide to rely on Him or to rely on ourselves.

Introduction

Isaiah was best known as a pre-exilic prophet who was called to warn both the Northern and Southern Kingdoms of the impending punishment they would receive unless they had a change of heart. The book of Isaiah can easily be divided into two parts. Chapters 1–39 focus primarily on the Northern Kingdom, Israel, and chapters 40–66 focus primarily on the Southern Kingdom, Judah. These two kingdoms, that once were united, had gone their separate ways. Both kingdoms turned their backs on God and ignored His commandments. Isaiah not only warned them, but he also extended comfort and hope as he spoke of a restoration and a return to their Jewish homeland. In the middle of their most troublesome times, Isaiah offered the thought of peace to both Kingdoms through a promise from God.

The Assyrians conquered the Northern Kingdom in 722 BC, and her sister Kingdom, Judah, was captured by the Babylonians in 586 BC. Their fates were sealed, so it seemed, but God had other plans. The trials these two Kingdoms endured are metaphorically spoken of in this text as waters, rivers, and fire. Because of their arrogant behavior, God's judgment was swift like the flowing flood waters, and their lives were scorched as if by a raging fire. However, God's mercy also shines through in this text as He promised, in the midst of this turbulent time, He would be with them.

Going Deeper

God warned both Kingdoms. They left Him no choice but to punish them for their disobedience. However, God never intended there to be a permanent separation between Himself and His people. The idea of redemption is as old as the first sin of Adam. When Adam and Eve made the choice in the garden to disobey God, perhaps they thought God would overlook their sin. They quickly discovered that God is a just God who demands obedience. Israel would later learn this same lesson. God demands obedience not only from individuals but also from nations. Disobedience (sin) separates us from God (Isa 59:2). God's love for His people goes very deep; His desire is to redeem those who have chosen to disobey Him. "Redemption was not a grandiose act for a huge mob. It was a very personal act by a God who calls each redeemed individual by name."[1] Isaiah wanted the people of Judah to know, even though they had turned their back on God, He formed them, He loved them, and He knew them by name. They still belonged to Him.

Notice God's choice of words through Isaiah as verse 2 begins. The first word we find is the word *when.* This word signifies that something will take place. He did not use the word *if,* which of course means something may or may not take place.

Isaiah also used common things to create a clear understanding of this warning. The use of water and fire are two things that can have adverse effects on each other. But if these things are not controlled, they can also produce devasting results. The deeper suggestion is that the waters can become raging rivers and flames can become a raging inferno, and both will overcome anything in their path, leaving behind nothing but destruction.

Israel and Judah had slowly allowed themselves to become immersed in their idol worship. They allowed their surroundings to influence them to no longer worship God the way He commanded their forefathers. Before they realized it, their sin of idolatry had consumed them, cutting them off from God.

Perhaps Isaiah's intent for using the phrase, *when you pass through the waters*, was so that Judah could reflect on the time their forefathers walked across the dry seabed when they were released from Egyptian bondage. Many of their forefathers saw the Egyptians destroyed, yet many of these same Israelites, once they were safely on the other side, had quickly forgotten it was God, not themselves, that saved them and provided everything for them. God wanted what was left of the kingdom of Judah to know the waters and the flames represented their time in captivity to both the Egyptians as well as the Babylonians. With their punishment now almost behind them, God was now preparing a way for them to return to their homeland.

The greatest news for Judah was that even though they were forced to go through the waters and the fire, God was still with them; He had never abandoned them.

Application

Israel and Judah's idolatry probably began slowly, before turning into an inferno of temptation and a raging river of sin. Still today, sin affects us in the same way. James offers us the formula that Satan uses.

> *Each one is tempted when he is drawn away by his own desires and enticed. Then, when desire has conceived, it*

gives birth to sin; and sin, when it is full-grown, brings forth death (Jas 1:14–15).

Just as God promised Israel and Judah that, even though they had sinned and were being punished, He was still with them and wanted to bring them back into a right relationship with Himself.

It is certainly true that life has a way of carrying you through what seems like rough waters and flaming fire. Perhaps you have heard popular quotes like "My life-guard walks on water." "If God brings you to it, He will bring you through it." These are cute and somewhat inspiring quotes, but they lack one thing; a promise from God. Sure, quotes like these seem to imply there is a promise of God, but it is not the same as what we find in Isaiah 43. What sets this text apart from such quotes (other than being the inspired word of God) is the promise God made in this text, *I will be with you.*

When we face our temptations, trials, and tragedies, we can neither avoid them nor go around them; we must go through them. However, it is important for us to understand that God's protection and presence are always near, regardless of whatever circumstances we may face.

Conclusion

Our character and our faith are refined by each trial or tragedy of life that we face. Often, these difficult events will not only shape and mold us, but they will also strengthen our reliance on God. James reminds us of this fact. *My brethren, count it all a joy when we fall into various trials* (Jas 1:2). In all my years of ministry, I have found very few who count themselves as being fortunate when they find themselves dealing with the hardships of life. However, I have seen many who have faithfully faced and endured such troublesome times. How does a person endure the trials and tragedies that life can bring? How does one overcome the negative feelings of fear and doubt that are found in these circumstances? Anyone who approaches such circumstances by trying to face them on their own will likely fail. A benefit of being a child of God is that, when you are faced with turmoil in life, a child of God can turn to the One that can help them through whatever they might be forced to face.

We often find an emotional or intellectual connection to certain passages through circumstances we have faced in life. Reading such a passage may cause you to reflect on a specific place and time. A passage such as this may even connect you to a happier time in life, or you may be reminded of a more difficult time. Isaiah 43:2–3 is such a passage for me. Each time I read this passage, it takes me back to a time when I found myself at a low point in my life. It was during this time I stumbled across this passage.

As a child of God, you have the assurance that you are never alone. There was a time in my life when I did not have that assurance. The choices I had made, the people I had chosen to surround myself with, and the situations I had placed myself in all contributed to my feeling of abandonment. I always enjoy reading the parable that Jesus shared with us in Luke 15 of the young man who left home, wasted his life away on frivolous things, and obtained many friends only to find himself broken and alone. It was only in his father's house this wayward son could find rest. Such peace and comfort can certainly be seen in the words of Isaiah 43:2–3. God's promise is why this is one of my favorite verses of Scripture.

> *When you pass through the waters, I will be with you; and through the rivers, they shall not overflow you. When you walk through the fire, you shall not be burned, nor shall the flame scorch you. For I am the Lord your God* ... Isaiah 43:2–3a.

This verse expressly addresses what many people go through daily: death, sickness, terminal illness, emergency surgery, chaotic home life, addictions, divorce, and various other relationship problems. These things (plus numerous other unfortunate circumstances) find their way into our lives, often at times when we least expect it.

What sets Isaiah 43:2–3 apart is the promise God made: *I will be with you.*

Discussion Questions

1. Life is constantly changing; list some passages that remind you that you are never alone.
2. How did the rebellious attitude of Israel affect its demise?

3. Can you share a time in your life when you finally understood just how deep the Father's love is for you as an individual?

4. Do people occasionally underestimate God's love for them? If so, how could Romans 8:31–39 help someone to see the depth of God's love?

5. Using Isaiah 43:2–3, what is the one major point you could convey to someone?

6. We have the example of what happened to a disobedient Israel. As our nation seems to slip further away from God, what are things we can do for our nation? How might 1 Peter 2:13–17 be applied to your answer?

Endnote

[1] Trent C. Butler, *Isaiah*, Holman Old Testament Commentary (Nashville, TN: B&H Publishing Group, 2002), 236.

Chapter 11
Isaiah 65:17–25
Baron Van der Maas

Introduction

IT'S AMUSING CALLING WALT DISNEY WORLD THE
"Happiest Place on Earth." In the sub-tropical climate
of Florida, the famous theme park is known for an
abundance of crowded walkways and an expensive
price tag. Despite waiting in long lines and tracking
25,000 steps on your pedometer, the theme park has
continued to be popular and a "magical" destination for
over 50 years. One way the magic still remains is in
Disney's innovation for imagination and creativity.
Walt Disney's vision for the future is clearly expressed
in his show, "The Carousel of Progress." The carousel is
a rotating showcase of the 20th century's modernization
through the technology of electricity. Placed in the
Tomorrowland district of Disney's Magic Kingdom
park, you can relax in the air-conditioned theater
listening to the production of "It's a Great Big Beautiful
Tomorrow." Disney knew, and the show proclaims, that

tomorrow is just a day away and that everyone can gain from innovations.

Disney's excitement for tomorrow shows the truth behind the human experience: Tomorrow is always just around the corner. Disney had an expectation and hope for what the future could bring. In Christian terms, Disney's eschatological view was that tomorrow will bring something more, and we patiently wait for that great future.

Digging Deeper

With Walt Disney's eschatology in the background of the discussion, we examine Isaiah 65:17–25. The expectant world illustrated in this passage is Isaiah's final vision of peace, prosperity, and joy expressed through the New Heavens and New Earth (NHNE). His vision includes three specific concepts. First is the vision of a high and mighty Creator! God is the only Creator who can make what the servants need (Isa 65:1–16).[1] Most likely, Isaiah is referring to the creation of the entire world (Gen 1). In his hope, Isaiah wishes that God would recreate everything brand new like He did on day one. Whether Isaiah envisions the destruction of one world for the existence of another, I do not believe so. The new creation takes the place of the former. It is refreshing that "the former things shall not be remembered ... ." Isaiah sees the old world as a forgotten memory due to the creation of the new. More likely recreation is used as a metaphor to describe a new beginning for people. It is a new beginning that God is starting for the people of Jerusalem.

The second key feature is the expectation of the holy mountain, Jerusalem, being the place of God's peace. Isaiah references himself from chapter 11, where peace is so prosperous that animals will live together in harmony and violence dissipates on God's holy mountain.[2] In the most imaginative section of this vision, Isaiah witnesses wolves eating with lambs and lions eating with ox. The equivalent of cats and dogs living peacefully together! However, this is the amplified picture of how great a sense of peace will encompass the mountain. God's peace will be brought by His own presence and gift. People will live and thrive, life will flourish, and even the animals will see opportunities to make friends amongst each other. How great a peace that can be!

The third is the expectation of life. Life is found in no one but God. But what do we mean by life? Isaiah does not mean just mere existence. Mere existence is a life of breathing, eating, and drinking just to get to the next day. Life means fulfillment and bounty, a desire to acquire families, build houses, plant and see the greatness of your crop, and a life where fear is not even on your mind. Isaiah illustrates a life where children live past infancy and adults live to be 100 years old and older. If you do not make it to a hundred, you must be accursed (Isa 65:20).

Through the three ideas of creation, peace, and life, Isaiah envisions not only a goal (in the future) but an expectation (a desire for today). Most readers come to the text with one of two feelings: these ideas are totally unachievable or these ideas can only happen at the end of time when Jesus returns. Envisioning it as a goal puts both of those views in perspective. Isaiah believes God can do it in his time, "For behold, I *create* a new heavens and new earth .... But be glad and rejoice forever in that which I *create* ..." (Isa 65:17–18 ESV). Isaiah believes recreation is something God is currently participating in, not just a distant tomorrow that will never be seen.

Application

Most people want a brighter future, better than their present situation. Right now, maybe you have a parent or child in the hospital or a son or daughter in the military, preparing for war on the horizon. Or perhaps you are burdened with debt, pain, anxiety, heartache, or a certain stress that looms ahead. The future has to be better, right?

Well the NHNE gives us the words of what we really want in our future. We long for God's presence, peace after chaos, a long life, and joy. For Christians, these are great promises. Christians hope for a big, bright, beautiful tomorrow. But how long, Oh Lord, until we get there?

There are two conclusions from Isaiah's vision for us today. First, any change in the right direction must be orchestrated by the will of God. Isaiah's vision is initiated by God, inhabited by God, and in tune with God. God cannot be separated from this new creation because He is entwined within it. God will answer before they call. He will hear while they speak, He is creating and making new for His servants. For the Christian, we must never assume newness is absent from God. So often we think that being in the right marriages, the right jobs, having the right number of children, the right hobbies, or any right situation will cause us to have a "right-eous" life. However, by ourselves, these changes will only be different and not made new with God. Isaiah's vision causes us to wish for God's presence, where He will wipe away every tear and make our worst nightmares disappear on a new and glorious day (Rev 21:1–5).

Second, we may not have to wait so long. The realization of the NHNE is experienced by Isaiah in his present day. The prophet knew that the current events of his day were changing. The events were most likely the rebuilding of the Temple in Jerusalem and the return of the exiles from Babylon. Today, we can change our present to be more Christ-like. God can change the future of any Christian's life. Paul says,

> Put off, concerning your former conduct, the old man which grows corrupt according to the deceitful lusts, and be renewed in the spirit of your mind, and that you put on the new man which was created according to God, in true righteousness and holiness (Eph 2:22–24).

God wants to make people brand new. He knows the former life is filled with deceit, malice, envy, sin, and corruption. The new man can live with righteousness and holiness, purity and sanctity (see 1 Cor 6:9–11). Once we were all sinners, but now we can be redeemed by the precious blood of the Lamb. A brand new future is available to anyone who calls upon His name. The future can begin today!

Conclusion

"There's a great, big, beautiful tomorrow, Shining at the end of every day. There's a great, big, beautiful tomorrow, and tomorrow's just a dream away." The human experience is wishing for greatness in the future. Preparing children and grandchildren for a future that will be handed down to them in progress and innovation. But God's future is bright, beautiful, and full of glory, that which this world knows very little about. Perhaps the second verse of Walt Disney's song is one that Christians today need to hear: "Man has a dream and that's the start, he follows his dream with mind and heart, And when it becomes a reality, *It's a dream come true for you and me*." The Christian future, in this life and the next, has a real impact on everyone in this world. The world needs the life of the Christian to be righteous, holy, and different from the rest of the world. Without the newness of Jesus, we will be nothing but just like the rest of the world. And that future is unfit for anyone.

Endnotes

[1] ברא (*barah*) is a verb only used in the Hebrew Bible to speak of God which means this is a divinely attributed action for Him alone. For other references of *barah* see: Isaiah 40:28; 42:5; 43:1, 15; 45:7, 18; 57:19; Amos 4:13; Ecclesiastes 12:1.1.

[2] The one minor difference is the lack of a messianic figure in Isaiah 65. For more information on the connection between Isaiah 11 and 65 see J.T.A.G.M. van

Ruiten, "The Intertextual Relationship Between Isaiah 65,25 and Isaiah 11,6–9," in *The Scriptures and the Scrolls: Studies in Honour of A.S. Van Der Woude on the Occasion of His 65th Birthday*, edited by F. Garcia Martinez, A. Hilhorst, and C.J. Labuschagne (Leiden: Brill, 1992), 31–42.

Discussion Questions

1. What are some key hopes Isaiah lays out for the reader? Why are these hopes important for Christians?
2. In what way can a Christian change today that can affect the future?

Chapter 12
The Covenant of the Rechabites
Jeremiah 35
Adam Richardson

Focus Passage: Jeremiah 35:17–19

PICTURE A GROUP OF NOMADS WANDERING AMONG the settled tribes in Canaan, remaining faithful to their forefather's covenant that they live distinctive lives from the people around them. As God rewards their commitment by granting that "a man from your house shall never cease to stand before me," you might be tempted to assume he is speaking about the Jews—but you'd be wrong.

Introduction

The setting of Jeremiah 35 could be described as Jerusalem standing with one foot in the grave, as the Babylonian empire rises to power under its new king, Nebuchadnezzar. In the ensuing chaos over several decades, conflicting messages about the future of the city come from all corners—some say God will deliver, some say God will punish. Jeremiah tries to convince the wicked king Jehoiakim and lackadaisical religious leaders to be aware of the dangers, but none will listen. If they did, they could be saved—so their stubbornness will lead to inescapable destruction. (As you can imagine, Jeremiah was the life of the party and a general joy to hear preach.) Regardless, he cannot stop because of the 'fire in his bones,' and he keeps finding more and more ways to insert himself into the public eye, hoping to convince people to listen.

So he invites a strange-looking group of wandering refugees who have just recently taken up residence near the temple to join him in an upper room of that magnificent (soon to be destroyed) structure for all passing by to see. There's not much to the exchange: he offers them wine, and they politely decline. Then Jeremiah turns to the crowds below and chastises them for not being more like this group of strangers. Their refusal to drink wasn't based on any law of God, but simply because several generations ago their ancestor, Jonadab, made a covenant with his family that they should separate themselves from the other people around them by not building houses or drinking wine or even cultivating the land with crops or vineyards.

Why should this short chapter that seems disconnected from everything else in Jeremiah's life matter to us? What secret history can we piece together from the pages of Scripture that show us the importance of this tiny group of outcasts? Can this isolated conversation with people we've never heard of enhance our entire understanding of the Old Testament?

Going Deeper

At first glance, this chapter just doesn't make sense, and that should make every reader stop and look a little closer. What is a 'Rechabite,' and why have they given up their nomadic lifestyle to huddle in the shadows of the "Big City Temple"? Although the trail goes cold several times, if someone is patient they can find a thread that traces this Gentile family all the way back to Genesis.

They explain for themselves how they came to the streets of Jerusalem in verse 11 of our chapter: They had been living in Samaria after the Assyrian army laid waste the Northern Kingdom over a hundred years before. But they knew they couldn't survive as the armies of Babylon occupied those same newly conquered regions. So, seeking strength in numbers, they come to Jerusalem. They still maintain their strange customs and habits, however, which must have made them stand out since few in the city even knew they existed before their arrival.

Why did these Gentile refugees make this decision? Each piece of this puzzle is worth its own investigation, but we'll hit the highlights and you can fill in the fascinating gaps. They are following the example of Jonadab, the ancestor they mention in their story. His full name, 'Jehonadab son of Rechab,' is given in 2 Kings 10:15, where we find out he's 'riding shotgun' for a fast-driving Jewish charioteer named Jehu waging a one-man war against Baal-worshipping bad guys Ahab and Jezebel. In addition to casting in his lot with the Jews, this Jonadab is the one who created a covenant with his descendants that they should forever distance themselves from the pagans around them by where they live, how they make a living, and even what they drink.

It didn't start there, though. Before him was Hammath, mentioned as being the 'father of the house of Rechab' in 1 Chronicles 2:55. Although there's a LOT going on in this genealogy, take note in Jacob's family tree at just *how many Gentiles* get 'grafted' in God's group. Judah married a Canaanite (v. 3). David's sister Abigail married an Ishmaelite (v. 17). Hezron's wife was from Gilead (v. 21), and Sheshan gave his daughter to an Egyptian (v. 34). At the tail-end of all this mingling with the surrounding nations, we read of the 'Kenites from Hammath, who was father of Rechab's house' (v. 55). So now, the Rechabites are linked to Hammath, who was also known as a Kenite. The Kenites were the original Gentile group to officially partner with God's chosen people.

These Kenites were already established in Canaan before Abraham showed up according to Genesis 15:19. And in Judges 1:16 and 4:11, one of the Kenites was Moses's gentile father-in-law! Because they were already familiar with the area, Moses would beg them to serve as scouts for the wandering Israelites in Numbers 10:29. Thus, the whole Kenite clan packed up and traveled in the wilderness with Moses. But again we should wonder: why would these Kenites be willing to join forces with followers of God?

The most compelling theory is that, as a group already living in Canaan when Abraham migrated there (Gen 15), they heard him and his clan speak of the covenant he had with Yahweh: the God who chose him to leave his homeland, travel to an unknown place, and serve Him there. Even after Abraham's great-grandchildren left Canaan during a famine to follow Joseph into Egypt, the Kenites somehow held on to this knowledge of Abraham's God, passing it along from one generation to the next. So, when Moses lives with the Kenites 400 years later and finds a burning bush, where he meets a God who says his name is Yahweh, his Kenite father-in-law may not have been as surprised as we might imagine! And they continued to realize something special about Yahweh, even when the Jews seemed to forget because we find them repeatedly teaming up with his people.

Application

An important lesson we should carry from Jeremiah 35 itself is the simple concept that God honors people who respect their vows (see Deut 23:21–23, Prov 20:25, Neh 9:38, and Eccl 5:4–5). The Rechabites standing before Jeremiah didn't refuse wine because God commanded them to, but simply because they were keeping a promise they made to their ancestor, and this show of faithfulness and loyalty pleased God. Nazarites voluntarily changed their lives to honor God by keeping vows not required by anyone else (Num 6). Paul made Jewish vows to God even after becoming a Christian (Acts 18:18 and 21:23). There is no reason to believe such vows cannot still be powerful demonstrations of our faithfulness to God today!

These special covenants should not be entered in the

hopes of coercing God to act in a certain way, or because we hope they will make us 'better' than those around us who do not undertake such a vow. They merely offer us the chance to show God in some small way our own decision to devote something specific to Him because of our commitment to Him. The vow may be temporary or permanent. In the same way that wedding vows represent a covenant binding us to our spouse, we may willingly choose to do the same with God, because it is obvious by His reaction to the Rechabites that He sees such devotion.

Conclusion

Consider this final thought: What grand scheme is revealed by this walk through history? How do the isolated snapshots of Jeremiah 35, 2 Kings 10, 1 Chronicles 2, and Numbers 10 challenge some of our preconceived notions about God's plan in the Old Testament? If you see how all the dots connect, you see the thin line weaving through the entire narrative of Scripture—a thread that encounters the Jewish people, *but isn't about the Jewish people!* The fact that a group of Gentiles continuously held on to loyalty to Yahweh is fascinating because they just keep on living in the background of the 'real' story and its heroes. And while everybody seemed to be ignoring or forgetting, God saw it all (Rom 2:14).

Didn't God tell Abraham way back in Genesis 12 that 'in you, *all nations* will be blessed'? Didn't He send prophets (not one, but two!) to the Ninevites? Aren't there countless prophecies about *all nations* flooding into the streets of Jerusalem for the chance to worship God in His holy temple? And in more specific ways, don't we meet individuals who defy the notion that only Jews were capable of recognizing the greatness of God? What about Ruth and Rahab? What about the host of Gentiles in David's "Mighty Men" like Uriah *the Hittite* (see 2 Sam 23)? Even in Jeremiah, we read of the first Ethiopian eunuch, a man named Ebed-Melech, who would also be rewarded for his faithfulness in orchestrating a daring rescue of Jeremiah from a pit right under the guards' noses (Jer 38).

It changes the narrative to realize God separated Israel for a reason, but that reason was not because He didn't have a continued connection to all the other people in the world. The New Testament accentuates that reality all the more—such as Acts 17 where Paul affirms that God "made every nationality to live over the whole earth ... so that they might seek God ... though he is not far *from each one of us*." We ought to appreciate the grandeur of God's overall plan, we ought to marvel at His ability to weave all the tiny threads we cannot see throughout history together into one amazing story, and we ought to worship Him for the climax of that story: that through *One Man* **all men** might be saved!

Discussion Questions

1. How does a better understanding or reminder of God's plan for all humanity assist us in reading the Old Testament?

2. In your mind, what are some of the more powerful examples of God's eternal consideration and plan for the Gentiles?

3. Why do you think God is so pleased in Scripture when people keep their promises/vows/covenants?

4. Do you think Christians should benefit from making vows—to other people or God? What kind of vow could one make, and what would be an appropriate occasion for such a vow? Does it have to be permanent, or can it be temporary (like Paul in Acts?)

5. In what ways does the lifestyle of the Rechabites parallel modern groups like the Amish or Mennonites? Are there lessons we can learn from those similarities?

Chapter 13
The Hebrew Boys
Daniel 3
James Stephenson

IF YOU HAVE EVER ATTENDED CHILDREN'S BIBLE classes during your younger years, you would have learned about Bible narratives like Daniel in the lion's den, Joseph in Egypt, the plagues of Egypt that God empowered Moses to perform, the crossing of the Red Sea by Israel under Moses's leadership, Samson and Delilah, and our story under current discussion—the three Hebrew boys, among others. These narratives have left an indelible impression on our minds right into adulthood.

Background

In the first chapter of the book of Daniel, we are introduced to four young Hebrew men whose names were Daniel, Hananiah, Mishael, and Azariah. They were from the tribe of Judah and were taken captives by King Nebuchadnezzar of Babylon during the siege of Jerusalem around 605 BC. Based on the request of

Nebuchadnezzar to Ashpenaz, his chief eunuch, these four young people who were among those chosen to serve the king after training, may have been of royal blood or of the nobility (Dan. 1:3). They were renamed Babylonian names whose meanings are not clear but may have been intended to honor a Babylonian god. Daniel, whose Hebrew name meant "God is my judge," was given the name Belteshazzar. Hananiah, whose name meant "the grace of God," was renamed Shadrach. Mishael meant "he that is the strong God," became Meshach, and Azariah, "the Lord is a help," became Abednego.[1]

While each of the Hebrew names honored the God of heaven the young men served throughout their lives, their new names replaced that significance and may have been to purposefully attempt to honor the gods of the Babylonians (Dan 1:1–7).[2] Interestingly, or maybe ironically, we tend to remember three of these outstanding Hebrew young men by their Chaldean names, even today (Dan 1:1–7), instead of their original Hebrew names. It seems safe to say that these Chaldean names were purposefully given to help fully assimilate them into Babylonian society. This was probably also designed with the intention of causing Daniel and his friends to shift allegiance to the Babylonian gods after whom they were named. That would have been a significant adaptation of Babylonian culture.

Digging Deeper

Assuming that the intent for the name changes was to initiate a change of allegiance from the God of their ancestors to the gods of the Babylonians, it did not achieve the intended goal. This is evident from the way the young men refused to defile themselves with the king's food as per Daniel's account in the first chapter of the book that bears his name, and here in chapter 3, where they would not bow to Nebuchadnezzar's golden image. Both instances in the young men's lives reflect a deep sense of trust in God and an unwavering commitment to serving the one true and living God whom they evidently revered. Their faith, at times like these, made the difference between obeying God and taking the easy way out.

The situation with the golden image was especially challenging because there was the element of the threat of death in a fiery furnace for not complying with the king's orders. Death by burning would not have been something strange during that era. There is a reference to this kind of punishment in Jeremiah 29:21–22.

> *Thus says the Lord of hosts, the God of Israel, concerning Ahab the son of Kolaiah and Zedekiah the son of Maaseiah, who are prophesying a lie to you in my name: Behold, I will deliver them into the hand of Nebuchadnezzar king of Babylon, and he shall strike them down before your eyes. Because of them this curse shall be used by all the exiles from Judah in Babylon: "The Lord make you like Zedekiah and Ahab, whom the king of Babylon roasted in the fire."*

Jeremiah had prophesied of the pending Babylonian captivity in chapter 25. In chapter 29, Jeremiah wrote to the exiles who were already in Babylon concerning how they should go about life in their new environment and how long they were expected to be there. Ahab and Zedekiah were delivering lying prophecies about the length of their stay in Babylon.

The indictment on these two men would have been to discourage false prophets from deceiving the people. The punishment was severe and administered under king Nebuchadnezzar. Therefore, the ordered punishment of death by fire of the three Hebrew young men was not unique or unusual.[3] In this Scriptural reference, the action of burning as punishment is given as if that was normal in the Babylonian era. The big difference here is that those in this text were deserving of punishment because they had prophesied lies. However, Shadrach, Meshach, and Abednego (using their Babylonian names) were innocent of any immoral or criminal behavior. All they did was stand up for their faith in the One true and living God whom they worshipped. They believed that the God whom they served was/is the God of heaven and earth, and that there was/is none like Him. This was embedded in their psyche because it was instilled in them from an early age. There seems little doubt that, at a time like this, they would recall to mind the words of Deuteronomy 6:4–9.

> *Hear, O Israel: The Lord our God, the Lord is one. You shall love the Lord your God with all your heart and with all your soul and with all your might. And these words that I command you today shall be on your heart. You shall teach them diligently to your children and*

*shall talk of them when you sit in your house, and when
you walk by the way, and when you lie down, and when
you rise. You shall bind them as a sign on your hand,
and they shall be as frontlets between your eyes. You
shall write them on the doorposts of your house and on
your gates.*

The instructions from this text suggest an assimila-
tion of knowledge that supports an oral as well as a
written tradition. Such would ensure the instructions
transcend generations to follow the primary recipients
right down to Daniel's generation and beyond. The
ancestors of these Hebrew young men would have done
an outstanding job in ensuring that future generations of
Israelites knew, and adhered to, God's statutes.

The three Hebrew young men made a stance on
what they knew was right. The threat of death by burning, as horrible as that sounds, could not shake their faith
in God. They would have been fully aware of the
Hebrew Scriptures that warned against serving pagan
gods. Moses, who is credited for writing the first five
books of the Hebrew Scriptures, known as the Torah,
covers this very teaching in Exodus 20:1–8; Leviticus
26:1; Deuteronomy 5:7–9, 8:19; and others. Further, the
reaction of these young men in Daniel 1, to not defile
themselves with the foods allotted to them by the king, is
a strong indicator of their knowledge of the Torah
regarding what they should and should not eat (cf. Lev
11). It is especially encouraging and uplifting to see the
determination of these young men who placed greater
value on pleasing God than on preserving their lives.

In retrospect, it would be remiss not to reflect on the attitude of the Hebrew youths that led up to the furnace experience. Daniel records (Dan 3) that King Nebuchadnezzar erected a golden image of sizable proportions *"in the plain of Dura"* (vs. 1) and summoned all peoples to fall and worship the image on (vss. 3–5) the day of its dedication. Anyone failing to bow in reverence would be thrown alive into a fiery furnace (vs. 6). According to verse seven, *"all the nations and peoples of every language fell down and worshipped the image of gold ...."* All, that is, except for the three Hebrew exiles. The officials of the realm informed King Nebuchadnezzar of their actions and reminded him of the proclaimed penalty for noncompliance (vs. 11). In a fit of rage, the king confronted the young men to confirm what he had heard. He offered them a second chance to comply, and this was their polite response.

> O Nebuchadnezzar, we have no need to answer you in this matter. If this be so, our God whom we serve is able to deliver us from the burning fiery furnace, and he will deliver us out of your hand, O king. But if not, be it known to you, O king, that we will not serve your gods or worship the golden image that you have set up (Dan 3:16–18).

This was a profoundly brave and resolute stance. They trusted in the ability and might of God to deliver them from the fiery death but interjected that, even if God chose not to deliver them, they would rather die a hideous death in fire than bow to his image. Basically, they preferred to obey God rather than man (Acts 5:29) because He is the ultimate power for all to obey. Whether or not God delivered them would not be a reflection of any limitations on God's part. They were good with what God's will was for them. They would rather die with God's approval than live in direct rebellion to His will. Someone said, *"One's attitude towards God's law is one's attitude towards God."* The reverence one has for God would be reflected in how one sees and relates to His Word. The deeper the relationship one has with God's Word, the deeper should be one's relationship with God. This appears to hold true for these young men. The reverence and devotion these young men had for God prevented them from going against His will.

Application

An application for today's generation is to remember, and to have this deep assurance in the fact and promise, that our God will never leave us nor forsake us (Heb 13:5). The confidence, dedication, and commitment that these three young Hebrew men demonstrated is a reflection of their belief and trust in the supreme God to stand by His promises. Mistrust comes easily, but trust demands something one can hold on to—for example, a track record. God had provided ample evidence for Israel to trust Him. He promised their forefathers He would build a great nation of their descendants, and He did. He promised them the land of Canaan as an inheritance, and He delivered. He delivered them from Egyptian bondage, made them walk through the Red Sea on dry land, sustained them through forty years journeying throughout the wilderness, and fought their battles for them while administering judgment on the people of the land. In the process, He gave them the land He had promised them, "a land flowing with milk and honey" (Exod 3:8, Num 14:8). The text in Numbers 14:8 is actually an excerpt from a song of deliverance that David wrote, glorifying God for His ability to deliver. God's track record speaks for itself, and the Hebrew young men would have been fully aware of that. No wonder they had such a deep sense of trust in Him. There is none like Him (Ps 86:8–10). Even Nebuchadnezzar had to admit that "there is no god who can deliver like this" (Dan 3:29). The implication of Nebuchadnezzar's statement would convey the unequivocal truth that there is no being anywhere else who could deliver like the God whom the Hebrew boys served.

The Hebrew boys were promoted after taking a tough stance for God. Their initial actions may have been interpreted by the king and his officials as rebellion. However, God viewed that differently. He blessed them for obeying under the most trying of circumstances. These men were already in service to the king, but they were promoted and given greater responsibilities. Nebuchadnezzar took note of their trustworthiness, their bravery, and their resolute stance. He would have wisely concluded that men like them would be an asset to him and the empire.

Looking back at Israel, one can see how God dealt similarly with them. God prospered them when they obeyed Him and renounced evil. However, when they rebelled and demonstrated little or no respect for Him and His statutes, they were met with divine judgment. Obedience results in rewards, but disobedience demands and invites consequences. That is a Scriptural principle that thrives consistently in God's dealings with His people. The following verses of Scripture reiterate this principle.

Proverbs 13:13 "He who scorns instruction will pay for it, but he who respects a command is rewarded."

Proverbs 16:20 "Whoever gives heed to instruction prospers, and blessed is he who trusts in the Lord."

Psalm 119:23 "Blessed are those who keep his testimonies, who seek him with their whole heart, who also do no wrong, but walk in his ways!"

King Saul was a typical example of the application of this principle. When he did not adhere to God's Word to him from Samuel the prophet, God rejected him as king over His people (1 Sam 15:23). There are tremendous benefits for obeying God but dire consequences for rejecting His Word.

Discussion Questions

1. What impacts you most about Shadrach, Meshach, and Abednego?

2. What lessons can you derive from Nebuchadnezzar's interaction with the Hebrew boys prior to and after the fiery furnace event?

3. How did the young men benefit from obeying God rather than the king?

4. What's so outstanding about the response of the Hebrew young men towards the king's request?

5. What may have been the driving force influencing the choices they made?

Endnotes

[1] Matthew Henry, *Commentary on Daniel: Complete and Unabridged.* (Electronic Edition, Logos Bible Software).

[2] *Baker's Encyclopedia of the Bible.* (Electronic Edition. Logos Bible Software).

[3] Frank Chesser, *A Portrait of God* (Huntsville, AL: Publishing Designs, 2019).

Chapter 14
Yet I Will Rejoice in the Lord
Habakkuk 3
Joshua Pappas

Focus Passage

Habakkuk 3:1–2, 17–19

One Main Thing

Looking at the world around us, have you ever wondered when God will do something about all the evil we see? Have you wondered why He continues to allow injustice, abuse, and corruption to run rampant? How can it be that the wealthiest, most influential people in the world are often the most wicked? Have you wrestled in prayer only for God, by His silence, to say, "No"? Have you labored in prayer, and the situation turned out worse than when you started? If so, know that God answered these tough questions long ago in His interaction with the prophet Habakkuk. If you learn what Habakkuk did, you will find cause to rejoice in the Lord even in the worst circumstances.

Introduction

We don't know much about Habakkuk. His name comes from the Hebrew root *Habaq*, which means "embrace" or "cling," which is fitting since the third chapter of his book finds him clinging to God in faith despite receiving a devastating answer to his prayers.

What we do know is the approximate date of his prophecy. He doesn't mention Assyria. The Chaldeans (Babylonians) are the new threat to Judah. Nineveh, the capital of Assyria, was sacked by the Chaldean king Nabopolassar in 612 BC. The Assyrian Empire crumbled three years later, and so did Judah's hope of revival when King Josiah was tragically slain in battle against Pharaoh Necho at Megiddo. In 606, the first year of Nebuchadnezzar's reign, the prophecy in Habakkuk 1:5–11 (the devastating answer to his prayers) began to be fulfilled when thousands of Judah's nobles were carried into Babylonian captivity. Habakkuk prophesied sometime between 609 and 605 BC.

When Habakkuk cried out to God (1:1–4), the moral situation in Judah was bleak. The Judaeans were overcome with idolatry. Injustice and immorality were rampant and—excepting the period of Josiah's reforms—had been for years.

God had already determined Judah's punishment, and the decision was final. Babylon would be the instrument of His wrath. Habakkuk was indignant about his countrymen's sins but was devastated to learn they would be punished by the wickedest nation in the world. He prayed as many faithful have prayed in evil times. God's answer broke his heart—but not his faith. Habakkuk chose, as all who would see the final victory must, to trust God, even if he couldn't understand God's answer.

Going Deeper

Habakkuk didn't receive God's answer passively. In 1:12–2:1, he replied with a series of moral questions he calls his "complaint." Simplified, they are: "How can it be right for You to punish the sinful by those even more sinful? How can You let the faithless continue to profit by abusing those helpless before them? Are You going to let this go on forever?"

The prophet's grief and confusion are evident, as is his faith. Note the trust and submission evident in his dialogue: "I will take my stand at my watchpost and station myself on the tower and look out to see what he will say to me, and what I will answer concerning my complaint" (2:1 ESV). In other words, "I've said my peace, and I know God is right even if I don't understand His judgments. I'm going to keep serving Him faithfully and wait for further direction." True wisdom!

God did give Him further direction. Habakkuk 2:2–20 teaches us much about how God rules the world. God revealed He would eventually destroy wicked Babylon and gave important warnings that are as relevant today as ever. Simplified, they include: "Trust that what I foretell, will happen" (2:2–3, Gal 6:9, 2 Pet 3:8–9). "The righteous shall live by faith," or, "If you would be righteous before God, and so continue to live now and eternally, live in continual faithfulness to God" (2:4, Rom 1:17, Gal

3:11, Heb 10:38–39). "Thieves will have all they hoard up stolen from them in turn" (2:5–11, Gal 6:7). "Those who live by the sword will die by the sword" (2:12; Matt 26:52). "God's judgments upon this earth teach us to respect Him and live by His word, and through them, He will accomplish His aims" (2:13–14; Isa 55:11; Matt 24:14, 28:19; Mark 13:10; Luke 24:47). "Drunkards and the sexually immoral will not go unpunished forever" (2:15–17, 1 Cor 6:9–11, Gal 5:19–21). "Woe to those who practice idolatry" (2:18–19, 1 Cor 10:7, Eph 5:5, Col 3:5, Rev 21:8). All these promises of judgment would fall on Babylon in God's good time, but they stand as warnings to all who follow in Babylon's footsteps in all times. A final command that ends the section is one with which many are familiar: "But the LORD is in his holy temple; let all the earth keep silence before him" (2:20 ESV). God is. God is right. God is powerful. God is never worried. God always wins. God is God. Trust God! It's okay to question Him, but humbly accept His answers. If He doesn't answer, humbly accept His silence.

This brings us to our focus, Habakkuk's prayerful psalm of trust and submission to God when he got what seemed to him the worst possible answer to his prayers. We need to be familiar with all of chapter 3, but let's focus on verses 2 and 17–19 (ESV).

> [2] O LORD, I have heard the report of you, and your work, O LORD, do I fear. In the midst of the years revive it; in the midst of the years make it known; in wrath remember mercy. [17] Though the fig tree should not blossom, nor fruit be on the vines, the produce of

the olive fail and the fields yield no food, the flock be cut off from the fold, and there be no herd in the stalls, yet I will rejoice in the LORD; I will take joy in the God of my salvation. GOD, the Lord, is my strength; he makes my feet like the deer's; he makes me tread on my high places.

Habakkuk was afraid, but he had learned the lesson of faith: Submit to God's will, and ask that it be done, not your own. He merely asked for mercy when the judgment came. God had said, "The righteous will live by his faith." Habakkuk answered in so many words, "If I'm broke, in debt, starving, persecuted, suffering famine, violated, even dying, yet I will exult in the Lord, I will rejoice in the God of my salvation." That's true faith!

Learn the lesson God taught Habakkuk. It's the same one Job learned through his sufferings (Job 13:15) and the Sons of Korah learned from contemplating their forefather's demise (Psa 46:2); the same lesson Jesus embodied on the cross (Luke 22:42, Heb 5:8). If you have everything without God, you don't have anything. If you have nothing but God, you have it all!

Application

1. God isn't opposed to us questioning, even challenging Him in prayer. Habakkuk questioned Him boldly and was blessed with wisdom and strengthened faith more lastingly valuable than peace and prosperity. Imitate the balance between boldness and humility in his prayer life.

2. When God's word foretells something, it will

occur. Don't let impatience lead you to unbelief. God has promised that His Son will return to rescue believers from this present evil age and draw us to Himself in joyful eternal life. Whatever we must endure to prove faithful, even if it means a violent death (Rev 2:10), is a small price to pay in comparison (2 Cor 4:17).

3. When it was clear bad would come to worse, Habakkuk didn't curse God; he worshipped. While all of us should pray for the world, our nation, our communities, and our families that we may live blessed and peaceful lives (1 Tim 2:1–3), if it's God's will for us to suffer, we should follow the prophet's example.

4. God has every right to use any tool at His disposal to accomplish His will. Everything is His to do with as He chooses, even you and me (Psa 50:12). If He wills the wicked should appear to triumph over the righteous for a time; never forget that it isn't over until it's over. On the Last Day, the unrighteous will perish, and the righteous go into eternal life (Matt 25:46). Stick with Jesus. He wins!

Conclusion

Habakkuk prayed as many faithful have prayed in evil times. God's answer broke his heart—but not his faith. Habakkuk chose, as all who would see the final victory must, to trust God, even if he couldn't understand God's answer.

Discussion Questions

1. How do we reconcile injustice and suffering in the world with the goodness and justice of God, as reflected in Habakkuk's dialogue with Him?

2. Habakkuk chose to trust and rejoice in God despite receiving a devastating answer to his prayers. How can we cultivate a similar attitude in our times of crisis?

3. When it feels like God is silent or His answers aren't what we hoped for, how should we respond according to Habakkuk's example? How can we question God while maintaining humility and faith?

4. Habakkuk struggled with the idea God would use a wicked nation to punish His people. How does the dialogue equip us with wisdom when we see evil seemingly triumphing in our times?

Scripture Index

Scripture Index

Scripture Index

Scripture Index

Scripture Index

Credits

Select Scripture quotations are taken from the NEW AMERICAN STANDARD BIBLE®, copyright© 1960, 1962, 1963, 1968, 1971, 1972, 1973, 1975, 1977, 1995 by The Lockman Foundation. Used by permission.

Select Scripture quotations are taken from the NEW KING JAMES VERSION®. Copyright© 1982 by Thomas Nelson, Inc. Used by permission. All rights reserved.

Select Scripture quotations are taken from the NEW REVISED STANDARD VERSION BIBLE, copyright © 1989 National Council of the Churches of Christ in the United States of America. Used by permission. All rights reserved worldwide.

Select Scriptures quotations are taken from the Holy Bible, New International Version®, NIV®. Copyright © 1973, 1978, 1984, 2011 by Biblica, Inc.™ Used by permission of Zondervan. All rights reserved worldwide. www.zondervan.com The "NIV" and "New International Version" are trademarks registered in the United States Patent and Trademark Office by Biblica, Inc.®

Scripture quotations marked HCSB are been taken from the Holman Christian Standard Bible®, Copyright © 1999, 2000, 2002, 2003 by Holman Bible Publishers. Used by permission. Holman Christian Standard Bible®, Holman CSB®, and HCSB® are federally registered trademarks of Holman Bible Publishers.

Scripture quotations from The Authorized (King James) Version. Rights in the Authorized Version in the United Kingdom are vested in the Crown. Reproduced by permission of the Crown's patentee, Cambridge University Press.

Scripture quotations are from the ESV® Bible (The Holy Bible, English Standard Version®), copyright © 2001 by Crossway, a publishing ministry of Good News Publishers. Used by permission. All rights reserved.

Scripture quotations marked "ASV" are taken from the American Standard Version Bible (Public Domain).

Contributors

Rick Collum (MMin 2018) is the minister of Mars Hill Church of Christ, Florence, Alabama.

Brad McNutt (Pursuing M.Div.) is the pulpit minister of Moulton Church of Christ, Moulton, Alabama.

Joshua Pappas (MMin 2019) is the preaching minister at LaVergne Church of Christ, LaVergne, Tennessee.

Gary G. Payne Gary grew up in Lincolnton, North Carolina, and entered the Army in 1977. Since then, he preached for two different churches for twelve years. He completed the Bachelor of Arts in Bible from International Bible College (now Heritage Christian University), the Master of Divinity from Harding University Graduate School of Religion (now Harding School of Theology) in Memphis, Tennessee, and the Doctor of Ministry from Fuller Theological Seminary in Pasadena, California. He deployed to combat zones four times during his thirty-six-year career, culminating as an Army Chaplain (Lieutenant Colonel).

He currently serves as the Chaplain Endorser for Federal-level Chaplains representing the Church of Christ. He also serves as a Shepherd at the North Broad Street Church of Christ in Albertville, Alabama. Gary and his wife Ellen have been married for forty-one years. They have three grown children, as well as two grand-daughters and one grandson.

Mark N. Posey currently serves on the Heritage Christian University Board of Directors. He is the pulpit minister of the Winfield Church of Christ in Winfield, Alabama.

Walter Rayburn (BA 2006) currently serves as the pulpit minister for the Owl Hollow Church of Christ in Franklin County, Tennessee. He has been in this position since 2010. He enjoys spending time with his wife Jenny and two children; Marley and Atticus.

Adam Richardson (MDiv 2020) is the preaching minister with the Petersville Church of Christ in Florence, Alabama.

Ralph Richardson (BA 2016) is the pulpit minister with the New Hope Church of Christ in Readyville, Tennessee.

James Stephenson (MA 2011) a minister in the Caribbean islands.

Lucas Suddreth (MDiv, Harding School of Theology - Memphis) is the preacher at the Dublin-Powell Church of Christ outside Columbus, OH. He has worked with congregations in Alabama, Tennessee, and

Ohio. He also has a beautiful wife, Rachel, and two children, Sheppard and Marceline.

Dewayne Tapscott (BA 1998) Dewayne Tapscott is an alumnus of Heritage Christian University and Athens State University. He serves as preacher for the Southwest Church of Christ in Huntsville, Alabama, and the Piney Grove Church of Christ in Winfield, Alabama in addition to his work as an Admissions Counselor with HCU. Coach Tap is also a committee member for the Alabama State Lectureship.

Thomas Tidwell (MA 2007) is an elder and preacher at the South Cobb Church of Christ, and the Director of the Marietta Campus of Georgia School of Preaching and Biblical Studies in Marietta, Georgia.

An Hong Tran (MDiv 2023) is the president of the Vietnam Bible Institute and a preacher at Dinh Hiep Church of Christ. He is married to Hoang Quy Thi Dong, and they have one daughter, Thu My Tran.

Baron Vander Maas (MA Harding School of Theology) is the minister at Mt. Zion Church of Christ, Florence, Alabama.

Onesimus Bible Study Series

The Onesimus Bible Study Series offers biblical lessons for personal or group study from alumni of International Bible College/Heritage Christian University. Each lesson flows from confidence in Scripture as God's inspired, living, and powerful word. Each respects the ongoing relevance of the Bible as it shows us God's heart and guides our service in the name of Jesus. Every lesson is designed to build faith and encourage Christian living.

Love of the Faith: Favorite New Testament Texts (2023)

Refreshing the Saints: Favorite Old Testament Texts (2024)

Confident of Your Obedience: Favorite Sermon on the Mount Passages (2025)

Joy and Comfort: Favorite Psalms (2026)

Also by Cypress Publications

Berean Study Series

The Bond of Peace: The Seven Ones from Ephesians 4. (coming 2026)

God Battling for the Hearts of His People (coming 2025)

Encountering the Gospel (2024)

Led by God's Spirit: A Practical Study of Galatians 5:22–26 (2023)

Majesty and Mercy: God Through the Eyes of Isaiah (2022)

For the Glory of God: Christ and the Church in Ephesians (2021)

Cloud of Witnesses: Ancient Stories of Faith (2020)

Visions of Grace (2019)

Instructions for Living: The Ten Commandments (2018)

Clothed in Christ: A How-to Guide (2017)

What Does Real Christianity Look Like? A Study of the Parables (2016)

The Ekklesia of Christ: Becoming the People of God (2015)

Radiant Study Series

CYPRESS

To see the full catalog of Heritage Christian University Press and its imprint, Cypress Publications, visit www.hcupress.edu

www.ingramcontent.com/pod-product-compliance
Lightning Source LLC
Chambersburg PA
CBHW031422120626
46545CB00006B/2224

Refreshing the Saints: Favorite Old Testament Texts is the second volume in the **Onesimus Bible Study Series** from Cypress Publications. It offers fourteen chapters from alumni of International Bible College and Heritage Christian University.

Readers will welcome the diversity of style and expression. Those who love the Bible will appreciate the respect for God's word as both relevant and authoritative. *Refreshing the Saints* is intended for both individual and group Bible study.

CYPRESS
PUBLICATIONS
An Imprint of Heritage Christian University Press

ISBN 978-1-956811-67-4
90000

9 781956 811674